A VILLAGE YEAR

A VILLAGE YEAR

ALAN C. JENKINS

Webb & Bower
EXETER, ENGLAND

Title page: Shadow of the past — from shoeing horses to sharpening lawn-mowers.

Published in Great Britain 1981 by
Webb and Bower (Publishers) Limited
33 Southernhay East, Exeter, Devon EX1 1NS

Designed by Peter Wrigley

Picture Research by Anne-Marie Ehrlich

British Library Cataloguing in Publication Data

Jenkins, Alan Charles
A village year.
1. Villages – England
2. England – Social life and customs
I. Title
941'.0091734 DA667

ISBN 0–906671–38–8

Composition in Bembo by Filmtype Services Limited, Scarborough, North Yorkshire.

Printed and bound in Hong Kong by Mandarin Offset International Limited.

CONTENTS

INTRODUCTION 6

JANUARY 7
FEBRUARY 21
MARCH 41
APRIL 53
MAY 63
JUNE 73
JULY 85
AUGUST 97
SEPTEMBER 117
OCTOBER 127
NOVEMBER 137
DECEMBER 147

BIBLIOGRAPHY 159
ACKNOWLEDGEMENTS 159
INDEX 160

INTRODUCTION

In one of the editions of *The Woodlanders*, Thomas Hardy said that he had received so many enquiries about the real name and exact locality of the village in which most of the action took place, that he might as well confess straight out that he hadn't any idea himself. Indeed, in an effort to oblige his readers he once spent several hours bicycling round the countryside in an attempt to discover the spot; 'but the search ended in failure; though tourists assure me that they have found it without trouble, and that it answers in every particular to the description given in this volume.'

With appropriate diffidence, it could be said that Hardy's words sum up the situation in *A Village Year*. Unless one were setting out to write a sociological study or some sort of guide-book, it is really impossible to describe exactly one particular or identifiable village; or, if not impossible, it would certainly be invidious if not positively dangerous. Not everyone likes his warts or bunions described in detail. It is similar to the case of the novel. No novelist describes in detail a certain individual: characters in a novel are a synthesis of different characteristics and traits.

Likewise, this book is an amalgam of various scenes, a blending of different atmospheres, though, if I can mix my metaphors thoroughly, with a strong basic plinth supporting it. I was born in the country and have lived virtually all my life in the country (apart from lengthy interludes such as the Battle of the Atlantic and sojourns with 'villagers' of a different kind, such as the Lapps), so I have not lacked material to draw upon; but writing about village life is like trying to pour a gallon into a pint-pot, and one can only be aware of how much has to be left out.

For even in a 'confined locality' there is always much activity, even action, albeit often of an inconsequential nature. But perhaps its inconsequence is part of its charm. In the words of Mary Mitford (who is quoted several times in this book), 'of all situations for a constant residence, that which appears to me most delightful is a little village far in the country; a small neighbourhood, not of fine mansions finely peopled, but of cottages and cottage-like houses, with inhabitants whose faces are as familiar to us as flowers in our garden; a little world of our own, close-packed and insulated like ants in an ant-hill, or bees in a hive, or sheep in a fold, or nuns in a convent, or sailors in a ship; where we know every one, are known to every one, interested in every one, and authorized to hope that every one feels an interest in us.'

Well, life has changed since Miss Mitford's times (she died in 1855, during the period of the Crimean War). But though no village nowadays can hope to be quite as insulated as hers, many people would echo her sentiments – witness the ever-increasing numbers who long to find their way back to the countryside.

JANUARY

As midnight strikes, both sacred and profane manifest themselves over the village. From the village hall come the bibulous and ritualistic strains of *Auld Lang Syne* as the dancers surge backwards and forwards in waves of *bonhomie*, which, for at least a quarter of an hour, everyone fervently believes will last forever, and the New Year is welcomed in with demonic shrieks and yells and a popping of balloons, while there seems to be a compulsive need to tear down the paper-chains that decorate the hall, as if they symbolized the chains the old year has bound us in.

Now Jeremy Dredge of The Lamb, who has run the bar, prepares for the final assault before his allotted licence runs out. Besides, he is anxious to get back to the pub and give a hand to his hard-pressed wife, for not all the locals have been at the dance, and The Lamb has an extension, too. And he doesn't want to embarrass young PC Keane, whose Panda is already in the village and who is by way of courting Jeremy's daughter, Black-eyed Susie. More to the point, the landlord is in constant fear and trembling of his mother, the formidable but diminutive Mrs Dredge senior, who has never forgiven her son for once, twenty years ago, being caught out breaking licensing hours. It was in the much lamented days of the village policeman (we shared ours with Great Noshington) and PC Trudgeon, suspecting the offence, had first secreted himself in the post office porch to keep watch; then, to make conscientiously sure, had borrowed a ladder, from which he had (no doubt with a grunt of satisfaction) gazed down through one of the pub windows and confirmed that young Jeremy, who had then only recently taken over as landlord from his deceased father, was indeed tippling with a few cronies. In those days £5 was no flea-bite, but what stung far more was the disapproval Jeremy ever after suffered from his martinet of a mother.

Even if the congregation at the watchnight service were composed of two handfuls of villagers rather than one handful, it could not hope to compete with the cacophony from the village hall. Yet there is a sort of dreamlike, almost mediaeval atmosphere in the softly lit church, still bedecked with the holly and ivy of Christmas (how far more dignified than those ghastly paper-chains), while the bescarved women, with the occasional male figure such as the Brigadier and Mr Deedes, the Parish Council chairman, valiantly strive to keep time with the vagaries of the organ, played with devoted unpredictability by Dan Figgins, the local postman.

For thy mercy and thy grace,
  Faithful through another year,
Hear our song of thankfulness,
  Father and Redeemer, hear.

But faint and modest though all this may be, there is no gainsaying the ascendancy that the church bells eventually achieve. In clangorous triumph they peal out from the crenellated four-square tower that looms against the murky sky and the church elms, whose branches in the sullen wind claw at the night like gaunt signallers sending out some weird semaphore.

Ring out, wild bells, to the wild sky.
Ring out the old, ring in the new,
Ring, happy bells, across the snow:
The year is going, let him go;
Ring out the false, ring in the new.

As yet there is no snow, but it is on the wind — a snarzling, dog-tooth wind, as Sam Dredge calls it, crouching on the pub settle and heating a poker red-hot before dipping it in his tankard to take the chill off his cider. ''Twill snow afore cock-crow,' he reckons, 'and anyways, if 'tis ordained, 'twill snow whether 'er be New Year's Day or Midsummer Eve.'

The dance has been a smasher, there is a gleam in the eye of Mr Pickup, the village hall treasurer (he drives the van for Switchers, the furniture people in the market-town), for folk have come from afar, as the uncouth revving of cars, blaring of horns, and crashing of gears prove in due course. But lively though they are, the strains of the dance band, the well-known group the Cider Apples (its moment of glory when it was featured on local television), cannot compete in impressiveness with the bells. Few sounds could be more redolent of the countryside, and as seventeenth-century Thomas Fuller declared in his *Worthies*, England was once called the ringing island, being renowned for possessing greater, more numerous, and more tunable bells that any country in Christendom, Italy itself not excepted. Moreover, he went on, the art of ringing requires a thoughtful and ingenious headpiece, for a *maximus*, a peal of twelve bells, for example, will afford more changes than there have been hours since the creation. (How many people realize that the everyday expression 'ringing the changes' comes from this?)

'A dozen o' bells? Reckon that 'ud make un's arms ache! Our six du bring on a wunnerful thirst, as 'tis!' says Reg Dredge — another of the innumerable cousins of The Lamb — captain of the bell-ringers, as he and his team hurry in for a last and well-deserved pint. The bell-ringers are an interesting cross-section of the village, illustrative of its varied population. Reg himself is a thatcher, another is a jobbing gardener, the third a retired bank manager, one is a farmer, yet another a milk-recorder, and the sixth, though by no means the least, is Captain RN, a retired naval officer.

They travel far and wide over the county, competing with other bell-ringers and occasionally practising on the bells of other parishes. In turn, if you sometimes hear a peal of bells in the village at some unwonted moment, it is because a bell-ringing team from Upper Noshington or Newton Maddock have come over to try out ours. There is a deep attraction in the bells, even for those who no longer go to church, as there is in churches themselves. To an extent it is because they were so much part of our lives for untold generations, while the church bell marked so many stages in human life and activity:

Men's death I tell
By doleful knell.

Lightning and thunder
I break asunder.

On Sabbath all
To church I call.

The sleepy head
I raise from bed.

The winds so fierce
I doe disperse.

Man's cruel rage
I doe asswage.

'They used to believe, you know,' explains Captain RN, after he has quoted that ancient verse, 'that ringing the church bells would break up a storm. They used to do it in France up to thirty years ago if a hail-storm threatened their vines. Pull the church bell like mad to send it away, anywhere, the next parish, as long as it didn't fall on their patch. But partly the thing about bells, you know, is their strength and weight and power combined with their special music. Why, a bell, it could crush a man like an egg-shell — and if you don't know what you're about as a ringer, it could haul you up to heaven quicker than you'll arrive otherwise, if you get hold of the rope the wrong way. But, d'you know, bells always put me in mind of the elephant. I did a spell in Burma after we'd kicked out the Japs. We had teams of elephants in the docks, shifting great baulks of timber. Those great brutes, five tons each, could have killed a man with a flick of their trunks or flung him to kingdom come. But their oozies, tiny little brown-skinned men, could do what they liked with them. Same as bell-ringers. A bell out of control, a killer, like an elephant can be. But, with an expert hand on the rope, there's music for you, eh?'

Long before cock-crow, as Sam Dredge had forecast, the snow was reeling down, drifting, floating, lazily almost it seemed, but with calm insidiousness. In Robert Bridges' words:

> Silently sifting and veiling road, roof and railing,
> Hiding difference, making unevenness even,
> Into angles and crevices softly drifting and sailing.
>
> And all woke earlier for the unaccustomed brightness
> Of the winter dawning, the strange unheavenly glare:
> The eye marvelled — marvelled at the dazzling whiteness;
> The ear harkened to the stillness of the solemn air.

The bibulous reveller, peering out, hastily drew the curtains across again and staggered back to bed. On the television aerials the jackdaws muttered disconsolately. Redwings huddled under the hedges. The village dogs snapped at the snow deliriously and the village children gulped down their breakfasts before rushing out into the never-failing wonderland snow always creates — and for a moment stopped in their tracks, 'fair 'mazed', as we say, at the transformation the village had undergone. As for the farmers, they cursed, especially those who had been caught out. No New Year's Day lie-in for them. For even those who had given up their milking-herds and turned to 'baby beef' sucklers had to plod forth to rescue their in-lamb ewes or bring their bullocks down to more sheltered parts, if they hadn't already yarded-up their beasts, for much of the parish lies across the slopes of Starvation Hill, renowned for its spectacular drifting.

However, there was one person who was unmitigatedly delighted with the snow, feeling it was God-given for the occasion (whose nature we will see in a moment). This was Mr Bragham. 'Only let it last until Monday,' he burbled, on his way to consult the Rector, wiping his steamed-up spectacles on the end of his scarf. 'Marvellously seasonal setting for it all!'

Now, Mr Bragham and his wife ('my good lady', he calls her on ceremonial occasions; 'my very much better fifty per cent' when he is in jocular vein) are signs of the times. He was a highly successful manufacturer of toilet requisites, as he terms it (in other words lavatory pans, bidets, baths, and so on), who retired from the Midlands to our village some three or four years ago, a fact made possible or at least practicable by the motorcar which has had such an effect on all our lives and on the character of the village in general.

Many ancient church bells were carved with appropriate inscriptions.
These two examples are from the seventeenth century:

When you die, Aloud I cry

and

Come when I call, To serve God all.

But at least these hungry sheep look up and *are* fed, unlike Milton's, which were swollen with wind.

'In the dead vast and middle of the night', with the village lamp and the moon keeping watch together.

Both Mr and Mrs Bragham have taken to country life with zest and, one might say, gratitude, after years of groping their way through Coketown. Mrs Bragham is a pillar of the Women's Institute and beams with greater pride and pleasure, I dare say, when she receives a first class for her bread-making or her preserves at the annual Flower Show than she did at her husband being made mayor of Coketown. Mr Bragham is even prouder, for he has been appointed Rector's warden and is forever thinking up good works for the benefit of the church. To see Mr Bragham of a Sunday morning handing round the plate (or rather the discreet little baize pouch they use nowadays, so that you can furtively drop in your offering without its being seen), is to be reassured of the solidity and permanence of the social fabric, whatever the uncouth noises off. He is likely to harbour mixed feelings when our parish adopts the growing custom of regular church-goers subscribing an annual sum to the church.

As well as being a fervent churchman, Mr Bragham is forever digging out old customs and superstitions. Perhaps all this is a reaction from a life consacred (to use an ancient word) to the material, even if a high-class porcelain one. Anyway, this year, to raise funds for the church, he has revived the custom of wassailing the apple-trees on Twelfth Night, a pagan insurance policy for a good crop.

For the occasion he 'borrowed' the orchard at Town Farm, the main source of Mr Slocum's little cider business. Mr Bragham had roused the Slocums' enthusiasm for the affair to such an extent that Alf, the eldest son, manfully forced a tractor up and down some of the apple-groves to make it possible for the spectators to trudge through the snow in their gum-boots. Admission was ten pence a head, for it was all heavily subsidized as usual by the ever-generous Mr Bragham — and even so, many were those, especially certain village boys, who crept in from all quarters evading Mr Watchet, the Parish Council clerk who, looking like some half-frozen Mr Jingle, was on the gate.

Indeed, to begin with, we all rather looked like that, and as many as possible huddled round the brazier at a corner of the orchard. In the flickering light, presently supplemented by the head-lamps of Alf's tractor, the Rector in his cloak looked like some gangling, nocturnal bird of prey that had landed in the orchard and was not quite sure of its bearings, while all around the snow was suffused with the dramatic ruddiness of the flames.

Mr Bragham, not surprisingly in view of his managerial days and his innate fervour, proved himself to be a considerable organizer. He and his wife had arranged with Mrs Slocum and two or three village women to prepare quantities of refreshments, mince-pies being the staple, but also the traditional (we had Mr Bragham's word for this) slabs of toast and sugar soaked in heated cider — of which latter there were generous quantities doled out from enamel jugs. All these were now distributed by a band of howlers, as Mr Bragham averred they used to be called in ancient times — half a dozen village children who, judging by their subsequent performance, were well named. Under the influence of Mr Slocum's potent scrumpy, the circulation was restored to our nether limbs and the slightly mumchance, self-conscious atmosphere was speedily dissipated. Rather like guests at a masked ball, we pretended to have difficulty identifying each other in the lurid glow. The Brigadier teased the Rector for having recourse to pagan practices for the benefit of the church.

But the purpose of the ceremony was eminently serious. Now into the aura of light stepped a gaunt figure, ghostlike in a genuine old smock, a treasured possession of Mrs Slocum. It was her brother-in-law, Dan Figgins, the local postman (and organist, as we have seen), who is a genuine spiritual descendant of all such as Dogberry, Bottom, Bullcalf, Feeble, and the like. He had been well rehearsed by Mr Bragham and now, attended by the howlers, and, shyly at first but with growing vigour, by all of us wassailers (movement being less petrifying than standing in the numbing snow), he began to stamp and prance around one of the apple-trees, chanting in appropriately bucolic fashion:

Yer's tu 'ee, ole apple-tree,
Be zure yu bud, be zure yu blaw,
And bring vorth apples good enow,
Hats vul! Caps vul!

— and with immense zest his acolytes or howlers or chorus echoed:

Hats vul! Caps vul!

so that the village dogs began to bark hysterically.

Dree-bushel bags vul,
Pockets vul and awl
Urrah! Urrah! Urrah!

continued Dan, his crazy shadow adding to the effectiveness of his performance. But the dignity of it was suddenly and rudely interrupted by an uninhibited curse occasioned by a well-directed snowball that landed on his neck out of the treacherous night.

For a moment it seemed as if the indignant howlers were about to break rank and seek out the foe, but a stern word from Mr Bragham got things going again and the theme was continued with a ragged 'Urrah! Urrah!' bolstered by all of us, including the Brigadier and Captain RN, while even the Rector had put aside any Christian doubts and was joining in like any good heathen.

'Aw 'iss, hats vul, caps vul, pudden basins vul!' continued Dan, after taking a swig from his jar of cider, and 'Urrah! Urrah!' faithfully echoed over the village roof-tops and the dogs went frantic.

But now abominable snowballs were bombarding us from several different points. Mr Bragham's howlers could no longer be controlled. They rushed out into the orchard to counter the assault and, judging by the war-whoops and chorus of abuse, they succeeded in driving out the unbelievers.

Nor was the ceremony by any means completed yet. We were not to be deterred. Solemnly Dan poured out at least a gallon of cider in to the roots of the apple-tree (alongside me I heard Sam Dredge suck at his teeth at such waste), while Mr Bragham himself came forward with a dish of the toasted whangs of bread and with equal solemnity draped them messily here and there on the lower branches.

Suddenly a shattering double bang split the air, set our ear-drums singing and made us almost jump out of our collective skins. Grinning zanily in the dancing light, Mr Slocum ambled forward, under his arm a still-smoking twelve-bore, both barrels of which he had just fired into the branches overhead, all part of the ceremony which Mr Bragham had so carefully researched.

'*That* is to drive away any mischievous spirits,' he positively glowed in his gratification at the evening's performance. 'I think we can now guarantee you a bumper crop of fruit, Mr Slocum, my good friend.'

'Ar, I shoulden wunner, midear, I shoulden at all wunner,' agreed Mr Slocum, and they shook hands in mutual satisfaction.

And as eventually the party broke up and we trooped home, Sam Dredge nudged me with cidery enthusiasm. 'My feet du be like reg'lar blocks of ice,' he said, 'but dang I, 'twur worth every penny of it all tu zee how pleased the old gent was, zno?' (Sam himself is eighty-five, nearly twenty years older than Mr Bragham.) 'What 'ee call it? Vesselling? Vancy that ole veller comen down here to

As set in time as the bedraggled badger and his victim, the cottage parlour still lingers on, a museum in miniature of a quieter age.

live and make zure Tom Slocum's zider apples du grow proper. That's what I du call a true Christian act, midear, eh?'

Three hundred years and more ago, Herrick wrote in his *Ceremonies for Christmas*:

Wassail the trees, that they may bear
You many a plum and many a pear;
For more or less fruits they will bring
As you do give them wassailing.

The snow-bones (as we call the patches of snow that remain after the rest has melted) lingered on so obstinately it was clear that more snow would have to come to fetch away these vestiges. One of the most stubborn of the 'snow-bones', incidentally, was the elaborate snowman the children had built on the village green. They had ingeniously set him in the stocks, with broomsticks to strengthen his legs. Now he gazed forlornly at The Lamb, as if longing, like some old tramp, to go in and warm himself. One of his tin-lid eyes had fallen out, his ancient top-hat (a present from the Brigadier) had to be fastened by a thatching spar, while at midday not only his nose but all his features tended to drip.

In due course come back the snow did, this time on a swirling, bewildering wind that drove it into gigantic, bizarre, sculpted shapes. Now it was more than merely decorative; with disconcerting swiftness, almost as one watched, it formed white barricades around every house and barn, separating one side of the village from the other and piling high the lych-gate of the churchyard, as if Death had taken a holiday and put up a 'No vacancies' sign. And the graveyard, guarded by its solitary yew, was one vast bed covered with the same deep undulating shroud. There was now no distinction between the hideous marble tombs of later times or the dignified, handsomely lettered slate headstones of the past or the humble nameless mossy mounds of forgotten souls. All the sleepers in the graveyard were united as never before beneath this marvellous white peaceful counterpane, which presently, when the storm had subsided and an innocent blue sky replaced the snow-murk, glittered with millions of tiny jewels.

'I do hope 'er lasts another week or so,' Cushy Doe, the sexton, said fervently, referring not to the snow but to Mrs Dunch who lay gravely ill, 'else 'twill go hard to find her a patch, I du reckon.'

'What a night,' we said, echoing John Clare's

What a night the wind howls hisses and but stops
To howl more loud while the snow volly keeps
Incessant batter at the window pane
Making our comfort feel as sweet again
And in the morning when the tempest drops
At every cottage door mountainous heaps
Of snow lies drifted that all entrance stops
Until the beesom and the shovel gains
The path — and leaves a wall on either side —*

For some the snow was sheer delight: the first fall had happened during the holidays, but now, splendid bonus, the new fall had cut off the village. The road

*John Clare paid no attention to punctuation, spelling or grammar

over Starvation Hill was blocked. The school bus couldn't get through! So the older children had two or three days in which to toboggan gleefully on the slopes of Town Farm Big Meadow, much to the chagrin of the primary age children who, in single file, could make their way to the village school between miniature precipices of snow. And several people were unable to get to work, whereupon one or two superior ones proudly got out their skis and imparted an Alpine atmosphere to the village as, bedecked with red pompons and gaudy sweaters, they hopefully visited Town Farm to see if there was any spare milk — for, needless to say, the Fleckham milkman could not get through either.

But those skiers did more than that, for a diabetic child, who had been staying the weekend with her grandmother, was stranded without her medicine, urgently needed. So the skiers ski'd all the way into the market-town and back, across fields and through woods, a matter not so much of distance as ploughing their way through soft snow, for which snow-shoes would have been more suitable.

Altogether there was a blitz-like cheerful matiness about the village. Because of their being unable to get to work, you came across people whose existence you had scarcely been aware of before and everyone became eager to lend a helping hand wherever necessary, clearing away the snow or filling scuttles for old folk such as Sam Dredge or Mrs Slee, and the sound of shovels scraping busily or of logs being chopped rang out over the place. One of the best worn tracks through the snow was to the village shop, which, fortunately, had only recently received its fortnightly supplies. If it wasn't quite like Mary Mitford's village shop, 'multifarious as a bazaar; a repository for bread, shoes, tea, cheese, tape, ribbons and bacon; for everything in short, except the one particular thing which you happen to want at the moment and will be sure not to find' – if it wasn't quite like that, it did at least fulfil some basic needs, from tinned salmon to tinned milk, from sliced bread to sliced ham. The homely bell at the door was rarely silent and many people who had scarcely ever patronized the shop before (except to buy stamps or post a parcel at the post office counter) began to appreciate its worth. Not that Mr Scales and his wife resented this 'convenience-shopping'. They were grateful for the snow that caused their cash register to play such a merry tune and philosophically hoped that some of the new customers would become permanent — especially as Mr Scales in normal times goes around the neighbourhood once a week delivering standing orders to some of his regulars.

As always, the snow was worst for the farmers and their stock. The once green fields of kale were for the moment inaccessible, although the wood-pigeons seemed to have a special technique of knocking the snow off the tops. The farmers anxiously eyed their stocks of hay, for last year's crop had been poor. At the first fall many had brought their animals in, and indeed Mr Slocum's bullock-yard had been fully occupied since before Christmas. It was now a steaming noisome mass of red beasts which stood in dumb resignation among a churned-up morass of straw and snow and dung. The bronzy, brassy Chanticleer led his hens into the shelter of the barn (none of your battery hens for Mrs Slocum), while as for the pigs, they complacently continued their normal routine of waiting for the next meal, for the only difference the snow had made to them was to sharpen their appetites.

It was the lambing that was most difficult, for this comes early here. Many ewes had to be dug out, especially in the fields on Starvation Hill, and after two or three nights' vigil, Mr Slocum and Alf were stubble-cheeked and hollow-eyed. Even where the sheep were snugly penned, there seemed more casualties than usual, perhaps because of last autumn's poor grazing, and Mrs Slocum's kitchen became a regular crèche, with half a dozen lambs being succoured.

She had plenty of help in this, for it was an exciting opportunity for some of

A scene that could be duplicated a hundred times all over the country. Although this particular church may be only some six hundred years old, a place of Christian worship probably existed on the same spot much longer — and before that, a pagan one.

the children kept from school by the snow — at least for the girls: boys from the Back Lane part of the village had declared war on those in the Church Square part and a running battle was in progress, interrupted only by meal-times and nightfall. Town Farm kitchen was the epitome of a rustic idyll — with the huge black kettle puffing its readiness to 'wet' the tea and a comforting warmth emanating from the Aga, cloth-wrapped hams hanging from the beams, golden onions keeping them company, a self-important clock ticking away on the mantelpiece flanked by two china King Charles' spaniels, a black cat and her kittens snugly ensconced against Watch, the pensioned-off sheepdog, whose head was stretched out on a clutter of gum-boots — while on the stone floor squatted four earnest small girls, determinedly administering the bottle to the woolly orphans, whose contented sucking proved that they needed no coaxing.

So many aspects of farming have become completely impersonal. The gigantic, terrifying machines have taken over, the hungry, lumbering combine harvesters, the monotonously rattling balers. No longer the merry haymaking days, with the farmer's wife and her daughter bringing out a picnic of seed-cake and cold sweet tea to the fields. No longer the dramatic moment as the last square of corn grows smaller and the farmer stands ready with his gun for the bolting rabbits.

But lambing has not been taken over. It remains one of the few intimate aspects of farming, which is fitting enough in view of the fact that shepherding was the earliest of man's farming activities, when he began to turn from being a hunter and gatherer.

We were almost sorry (not quite, and certainly not Jeremy Dredge, whose beer supplies were running short for The Lamb had become more of a club than ever — darts, skittles, dominoes, take your choice alongside an ever welcoming fire) that the siege of the village was soon over. And long before the District Council had sent out a snow plough to clear the road over Starvation Hill, Alf Slocum and one or two other resolute farmers had forced a way with their tractors through the Drover's Road, a track which runs from the village to the main road, for the milk-tanker had been unable to get through and the farmers were desperate to get rid of their milk.

And as soon as they got through the postman's cheerful red van came bumping and stuttering along, followed by a police Range Rover bringing one of the Fleckham doctors to visit Mrs Dunch.

FEBRUARY

Undoubtedly the village — any 'real' country village — does provide an atmosphere in which the individual can breathe more freely, not merely physically but spiritually as well. As a result characters stand out far more prominently. Of course, these exist in the town — practically all Dickens' characters were townsfolk, from Mrs Jellyby who was so concerned for the welfare of the natives of Borrioboola-Gha, to the odious Uriah Heep, ever so 'umble — but they are nowadays submerged by sheer numbers. You can walk down Oxford Street with shaven pate and tinkling bells and chanting incomprehensively without a head being turned. Even a streaker scarcely rates a shrug.

But in the village everything is far less anonymous, far more apparent. 'Country people *know everything*', wrote William Cobbett, 150 years ago. 'If you have ever made a *faux pas*, of any sort or description; if you have anything about you, of which you do not want all the world to know, never retire to a village, keep in some great town.' Or, as Mr Slocum observed in the pub the other day, 'Why, bless'ee, midear, folks du know what'ee have had for breakfast afore you've even a-drawn up chair to table.' To put it pictorially, town life is as if conceived by Lowry — nameless, sticklike manikins going about their antlike affairs; country life, village life, is as if drawn by Breughel — the characters stand out more vividly, more dramatically, warts and all — and a good few bunions to boot. In fact, to a great extent you could say that the village nowadays simply consists of characters. The majority of people live here from choice, not necessity. There is no real binding force: the school, already only a primary one, will soon disappear; the church's influence everywhere has diminished; the farms, even the large ones, are no longer the great employers of the past, when a score of men worked at the hay-cut, and half a dozen carters was not exceptional.

We have our meed of characters: Captain RN, that gallant naval officer who has such a passion for old machines and implements and who, as we have seen, is a member of the bell-ringers' team; the Rector himself, gauntly handsome, straight out of a Three Nuns advertisement and always ready to delay evensong to argue with the most uncompromising atheist if he meets him in the village street; Miss Flora Bundy who rescues all manner of orphaned creatures, from jackdaws that have tumbled down a chimney to badger cubs whose parents have been butchered; or that shy young couple at Nut-tree Corner who are striving to eke the good life out of three acres.

But undoubtedly in any public opinion poll, Sam Dredge would come high if not top of the village pops. Even newcomers, eager to be accepted, soon realize that he is someone to be known, quite as much as the Squire. Great-uncle of Reg the thatcher (who, by the way, is captain of the village cricket team as well as of the bell-ringers), Sam is a pint-sized little man, neat, polished like mahogany, always composed. His cap, rigidly straight, is always firmly clamped on his small, alert head, not a fraction out of true, as if he was anxious to stop himself growing any more than his five foot three inches. Except for an occasional funeral, he never goes to church, so the matter does not arise in that connection; nor can I speak of his sleeping habits. Otherwise, that flat cap is invariably in place — when he is gardening, or at his own table, or by the fire, or at a parish meeting, or 'strolling', as he calls it, or now, sitting in The Lamb drinking the first of one or two 'jars' of cider.

We are proud of Sam. He is our oldest inhabitant, eighty-seven next year, and the unofficial parish historian — verbally, at least, for I doubt if Sam ever put pen to paper, other than to sign his name, once he left school and took up his first job scaring birds. But inside that small cranium he has stored up an inexhaustible fund of information: of parish events stretching back to the turn of the century; of epic matches; of forced sales; or catastrophic droughts, fearful winters; births, deaths, marriages; cases of assault and battery; the names of fields; who was captain of the bellringers when *the* queen died, and so on. Frequently Mr Watchet the parish clerk has consulted Sam about some uncertain point in parochial affairs.

Moreover, Sam comes of a notably long-lived family. His father, also Samuel, lived well into his eighties. And *his* father, inevitably another Samuel, was born in the year of Waterloo. No stones mark their graves, but Sam can point out the humble mounds where, he says, they lie, draped with a pall of moss.

But we cherish Sam for other reasons — for his imperturbable friendly character, his incredible spryness, for he still follows the hunt with an energy and enthusiasm augmented by an unparalleled knowledge of short cuts and the ways of the 'red thief'. In addition, we have a sly admiration for the fact that Sam is an inveterate poacher — perhaps not quite so inveterate these days, but we know full well that when Sam goes 'strolling', it isn't just to smell the flowers.

On the particular evening in question, we had abrupt evidence — well, not evidence, but a hint of this. Sam was preparing for his nightly game of dominoes with Cushy Doe, the sexton, and had just begun to shuffle the 'bones'. The talk was of gardens — Reg had got his broad beans in, Fred Marks swore he had walked ten miles stamping his onion bed suitably hard, ready for the setts — when into The Lamb stumped Albert Comstock. A sudden, momentary hush fell upon the few of us present, for it was fairly early on. Fred paused with a dart up-raised. Reg clicked his tongue irritably as he snapped the chalk with which he was marking the score. Black-eyed Susie paused in the act of drawing a pint.

To begin with, Mr Comstock is a Great Noshington man, and, like so many villages all over the country, 'us' and Noshington don't get on. Once upon a time, I have been assured, a man from our village could not walk down Noshington main street without the risk of getting in a brawl. Mods and rockers have nothing on old village feuds, which date back to tribal days. Second, Albert Comstock is gamekeeper to the 'syndicate', a high-powered shooting enterprise that rents or owns a large property spreading over part of two parishes. Landowners are one thing, syndicates quite another. Nobody likes them. They are anonymous, faceless, unfeeling, always ready to make trouble through their stooges. And Comstock himself, like most of his fraternity, is a taciturn, 'separate' man whose uncompromising eyes seem to suggest that he regards his fellow men (bosses excepted) as on a par with other vermin such as magpie, crow, hawk and stoat.

He put one in mind of Mellors in *Lady Chatterley's Lover*, carrying with him a 'swift menace', and he had the same red face, red moustache and blue, impersonal eyes. As he takes his drink — whisky, of course — from the aloof Black-eyed Susie, there is an air of hostility almost as tangible as the blue tobacco smoke wreathing about the bar, and the game of darts has resumed with an expressive and collective grunt. Sitting at one of the scrubbed tables, Sam doesn't blink an eyelid, but goes on demurely sipping at his mug and waiting for the sexton to turn up, although it is instinctively obvious that he is the cause of Albert's unexpected visit.

The gamekeeper straddles his booted feet wide apart, a swaggering brave conscious of being in enemy territory, wipes his moustache, takes his time lighting a cigarette, blows forth a contemptuous blast of smoke, and fixes Sam with a double-barrelled number five shot stare as if he was squinting along a gleaming Purdey twelve-bore.

'I see'd you sneaking out of Darnley Copse yesterday morning,' he says, while half a dozen pairs of eyes regard him covertly. 'Don't let it happen again, grand-dad. You might do yourself an injury. That's strictly private property.'

'Nobody calls me grand-dad,' Sam replies, evenly, although his back stiffens imperceptibly, ''cept for my grand-childer. What's more, midear, I'd been strolling along the public footpath. Looking for Lent lilies. They'm early this year.'

'That there footpath has been closed these twenty years. It was never registered,' Mr Comstock ground on, slapping his glass down. 'Same again.'

''Tidden so,' breaks in Reg, missing a double top as a result. 'That case has never been settled. Darnley footpath is still open. We be gooing to include it next time we beat the bounds.'

The gamekeeper blandly ignores this and the supporting murmur.

'I'm only here to warn you, *Mister* Dredge,' he continues, pointedly counting his change, to the evident displeasure of Black-eyed Susie. 'Don't let it happen again or you'll find yourself up before the beaks. And not for the first time, that's for sure!'

'What about they sparrow-hawks and owls on your gibbet, then?' demanded Sam, fiercely. 'Protected species, they are. *You*'ll find *yourself* up before the same bench. And I woulden mind betting you use pole-traps, too!'

'Might's well leave the door open when 'ee gooes,' Fred addressed the dartboard, as, fairly soon afterwards, Comstock stumped off. But as he did open the door, the keeper stepped back smartly and his whole manner changed, for in came the Brigadier and Comstock practically stood to attention.

'Don't often see you here, Comstock,' grunted the Brigadier, well aware of the atmosphere.

'No, sir. Nice evening, sir,' he said, touching his cap, and vanished into the night.

'What have you been up to this time, Sam, you old rascal?' the Brigadier inquired, stooping his tall figure to avoid a beam as he took up his usual position in front of the fire.

'Ah, well, midear,' Sam said, as he resumed his seat after fetching another jar of cider. 'I suppose 'tis only his job. But they'm a hard lot, gamekeepers. Bred in the bone. I an't never met a keeper whose Dad wasn't one before 'un. I woulden be surprised if that fellow's grandma weren't one, too, zno? But it must have been real wicked in the old days, when folk used to *have* to poach to purvide their little 'uns with a taste of meat. No butcher's meat for they. Coulden afford it. My own gran'dad used to tell I some fearful tales when I was a nipper not so high's this bench — '

For when that particular Samuel Dredge had been a youth, mantraps were still in use, immense, brutal gins which could maim a man for life, while hidden spring-guns could kill him; both continued to be used even after they had been declared illegal in 1827. The decade or two following Waterloo were hungry years, made worse by the infamous Corn Laws which artificially kept up the price of bread for the benefit of the farmers. The English peasant of the eighteenth century had been better off than his descendants. But all this coincided with another factor, quite apart from the economic.

We hear a lot about the mythical Captain Swing, leader of the farm-labourers who were fearful for their jobs because of the introduction of the threshing-machine. Ricks were set on fire and machinery smashed; two thousand men were tried by the courts, nineteen were hanged, and hundreds exiled. But, as E.W. Bovill put it:

> The unhappy but short-lived consequences that flowed from the invention of the threshing-machine paled before the long-drawn misery that the invention

If not exactly Shakespeare's 'babbling gossip of the air', at least this is the exchange of some juicy piece of village scandal, perhaps. Henry Fielding said that scandal was one of the best sweeteners of tea.

Even the doorstep delivery of milk may be ended if the EEC has its way and 'long life' milk becomes the rule, making still more tenuous the link between farm and household.

Every village had its heroes, especially in the First World War, when they went from plough, smithy and manor house alike. Many never returned, as local memorials testify, their names augmented by those of heroes from the Second World War.

of the flint-lock gun brought to rural England. For more than half a century much of the countryside was wracked by a bitter war, costly in human life and happiness, provoked by the sporting gun having given to wild game an importance it had not known before. There is no greater proof of the stability of the social structure of the English countryside than its having survived unscathed a merciless struggle in which an infinitesimal privileged minority fought to retain an exclusive right to what the whole of the rest of the community were convinced was a gift from God to be enjoyed by all.

'A wonderful lot of working men don't believe as there's any harm in poaching. We never read that in the Testament, nor yet in the Bible. We always read there, that the wild birds is sent for the poor man as well as the quality.' That was a farm-worker speaking in Regency days. It could just as well have been Sam.

As for the poachers themselves, of course there were many who poached for profit; but the majority poached out of dire necessity, a fact typified by a Surrey labourer Cobbett mentioned in *Rural Rides*. He asked the man how he could possibly manage on the pittance of half a crown a week that the parish paid him for breaking stones. 'I poach,' the man answered. 'It is better to be hanged than starved to death.'

And hanged many of them were, while even more were transported to Australia. Sometimes Bow Street runners were brought into the countryside in the war against poaching. One of these predecessors of the police force once boasted that within four months he had been successful in having twenty-two men transported. 'The gangs,' he wrote, 'are connected together at different public houses, just like a club; they are all sworn together. If the keeper took one of them, they would go and attack him for doing so.'

For hungry men are desperate men and violent pitched battles often took place. Sydney Smith wrote on one occasion that 'there is hardly a gaol-delivery in which some gamekeeper has not murdered a poacher, or some poacher a gamekeeper'. And this, as an example:

> At the very beginning the blacksmith, their ablest man and virtual leader, was knocked down senseless with a blow on his head with the butt end of a gun. Immediately on seeing this the two famous shearers took to their heels, and the young labourer followed their example. The brothers were left but refused to be taken, although the head gamekeeper roared at them in his bull's voice that he would shoot them unless they surrendered. They made light of his threats and fought against the four, and eventually were separated. By and by the younger of the two was driven into a brambly thicket where his opponents imagined that it would be impossible for him to escape. But he was a youth of indomitable spirit, strong and agile as a wild cat; and returning blow for blow he succeeded in tearing himself from them, then after a running fight through the darkest part of the wood for a distance of two or three hundred yards they at length lost him or gave him up and went back to assist the head keeper and his second against the other man. Left to himself he got out of the wood and made his way back to the village. It was long past midnight when he turned up at his father's cottage, a pitiable object covered with mud and blood, hatless, his clothes torn to shreds, his face and whole body covered with bruises and bleeding wounds.*

But not all poachers were workingmen. Colonel Peter Hawker was an inveterate poacher who once even stopped the mail-coach in which he was riding to dive into some noble estate and have a bang at a covey of partridges he had

*W. H. Hudson, *A Shepherd's Life* (1910)

Some home produce here — eggs, rabbits and pasties — but those other items have come from foreign climes and in the days before swift transport were virtually unknown to former generations.

spotted. On another occasion he persistently poached the coverts of his neighbour, Lord Portsmouth. When the noble Lord finally became fed up with these depredations and set his men to keep watch, Hawker simply 'got some fellows with guns and pistols to draw their attention elsewhere while we attacked their grand preserve; everything was arranged agreeably to a military plan which answered so well that we got two hours' glut of their pheasants, twenty-eight of them in fact'.

'Ah, maybe so, midear,' Sam frowned a little when I told him of this. 'A gentleman, he could do things just for the devilment of it, begging your pardon. But when gran'dad was a boy, folk poached because their bellies were empty. Gran'dad once told I that he got 'zactly sixpence a day for a long whiles. But he didden hold with burning no ricks,' he added.

'Ah,' sighed the Brigadier, contemplating the lacework of froth in his empty tankard. 'England's green and pleasant land, eh, what?'

'The agricultural rate bean't all that famous even now,' muttered Fred, landing a dart with a satisfying doink on the board. 'Reckon we'd do best to join in with the TGW.'

Soon after this, returning from the market-town, I came across Sam Dredge leaning on the parapet of the hump-backed bridge spanning the river near Old Mill.

'They're running!' he said, his mellow-apple face glowing with excitement as I wound down the window to offer him a lift. No need to ask who 'they' were. I got out and joined him in time to catch a glimpse of a superb silvery muscular body curving out of the busy water and flinging itself at the weir. Again and again that salmon would make the leap — and here there was no fish-ladder to help it — in its urgent need to get upstream, far upstream, even into the shallow little ditches of the river's source, and, with its chosen mate, perpetuate its kind. It seemed to bend its head to its tail, and then to fling itself forwards and upwards, 'much as a bit of whalebone whose ends are pinched together spring forward on being released', as Charles St John once described it.

'Bain't they downright beauties, eh?' Sam shook his head appreciatively as, reluctantly, he presently slipped into the car and we drove off. 'Did'ee ever see the like? Lissome as a maid! Strong's a horse!'

Although he was genuinely filled with wonder at the works of nature, he would cheerfully have plunged a pitchfork into one of those salmon — as he had done on innumerable occasions in the past, by the light of a torch made of oil-soaked rags. He put me in mind of Mary Mitford's Tom Cordery (another of the same ilk equipped with a 'huge inside pocket') who had the 'remarkable tenderness for wild creatures which is so often found in those whose sole vocation seems to be their destruction in the field'.

'Corbugger it, midear,' Sam pursed his lips regretfully, ''tis nigh on ten years since I last speared a salmon.'

'Yes, I remember,' I nodded. 'Bad luck being caught like that. Hefty fine, too.'

The old man glanced sidelong at me, with a little quirk on his lips. He was in an expansive mood.

'Shall I tell'ee some'at, midear? But don't 'ee never go blabbing to a soul. But I trust 'ee, zno?'

And he proceeded to tell me how, when his grand-daughter Rosie was going to be married to Len Poskins, the carpenter over to Whiterock, he had promised there would be salmon for the wedding-breakfast ('Though why, my dear soul, they du call it a breakfast when 'er takes place later nor dinner-time and volks stuff themselves to busting-point!'). It went without saying that the salmon would be 'obtained' by gran'dad, for the Dredge family was mighty proud of Sam's reputation.

But alas! as Sam admitted, the old flair had been dimmed, the old legs 'didden taken kindly any longer to perishing cold river water. 'Twould 'a fruzzed the feet off an Eskimo.' He had no luck; worse, he had been embroiled in an unpleasant scene with the river-bailiff who had somehow got his trousers wet. But Sam could not disappoint little Rosie, who had set her heart on that salmon wedding-breakfast.

So, after much inward wrestling, he had gone off next day to town, in the motorbike and sidecar he still chugged about in at that time, and purchased, *purchased*, mark you, a sizeable salmon from Yates the fishmonger. It isn't difficult to imagine how that went against the grain.

Back in the village, Sam found the river-bailiff and PC Trudgeon waiting for him. A complaint had been made, the constable intoned, going on to talk about physical assault and other dire charges — at which time that cheeky varmint of a river-bailiff had actually dared to open the lid of the sidecar, in which he discovered the salmon.

'Look at it!' the dunder-headed bugger had screeched like some old barn owl pouncing on a mouse. 'Eight pounds or I'm a Dutchman! Never seen such salmon in the river!'

The policeman was wetting his pencil and Sam was anticipating with glee the moment when he would make that interfering little dung-beetle of a river-bailiff look a prize idiot. He would like to see that fellow's ugly jizz when he told them he had bought the salmon and could prove it (even though he winced at the price he had had to pay).

And then he had a double-take, although he did not call it that. ''Twas a fence I shied at, actually,' he said. How could *he*, Sam Dredge, admit to having failed in his night's foray and gone off and bought the fish . . . His reputation would be shattered. He would be the laughing-stock of the village. And Rosie would take it all to heart far more than not having salmon at her wedding-feast.

'OK, Percy,' he had said to the policeman. 'Write 'un all down.'

Cost him a packet; he sucked his teeth in bitter memory, as we approached the village. ''Twir that old basket Major Trypington on the bench in those days. Now, mind, midear, don't 'ee breathe a word! 'Twoulden du, zno?'

The price of pride had been pretty high, but at least Sam's reputation had been saved.

It is not mere romanticizing that makes the idea of the poacher as a sort of folk-hero linger on. Our Sam is very much part of village history. He represents a vital tradition in the countryside symbolizing, at a great distance, the cruel struggle that many country people, generations ago, had to wage simply to keep body and soul together. But his modest activities were bow-and-arrow stuff compared with the professional poaching that goes on today, especially in connection with the salmon. With their poisons and explosives, collapsible boats and schnorkels, their lightweight monofilament nets which, even if a fish fights its way through, cause net burns on which fungus disease so easily develops, modern poachers are vicious and unscrupulous, lured on by the easy picking of £4 a pound, and against whom river-wardens fight an unequal battle.

In connection with all this, we recently had a living echo from the past. Sam had often talked about his Australian cousins (and of course they are also related to the other Dredges in the village), and one day he came proudly into The Lamb accompanied by a bronzed, fair-haired young man, ludicrously tall in comparison with the old man. His name was Dredge, too, and his family had emigrated from the village several generations ago. It was a family tradition that the distant father of that branch of the Dredges had been transported for poaching and it is perfectly feasible that this was so.

But whether transported or quitting his homeland freely, it was the English villager who largely populated the colonies in general. 'We have no gamekeepers and more privileges,' wrote one rural emigrant in a letter home. The reception accorded to Mr Comstock in the pub was a throw-back to an historic attitude on the part of the villager, although nowadays real hatred has changed into mere dislike for the gamekeeper.

Fortunate is the village whose church tower or farm buildings provide a sanctuary for barn owls. These birds are the most valuable of all in man's economy, but they have suffered greatly in past years, partly through the widespread use of poisons that have killed off so many of their natural prey.

Nothing is new, not even the Chinese take-away. Flora Thompson quoted a village shop, one hundred years ago, that sold penny plates of cooked prunes and rice to the village children every evening.

Football gives men an opportunity not only to display their skill but also to indulge in the physical encounter they enjoy. And unlike hunting, cricket, tennis, shooting or fishing, it needs virtually no equipment — simply a ball and somewhere to play.

RIGHT
For many people this scene would epitomize their hopes for 'a calm world and a long peace'. They would not think such a condition a canker, as Sir John Falstaff did.

Steadily since the eighteenth century, when they were first brought over from Holland, Friesians have become the most popular milking cow in English farming. A Friesian cow will yield 2,000–3,000 gallons of milk in a lactation.

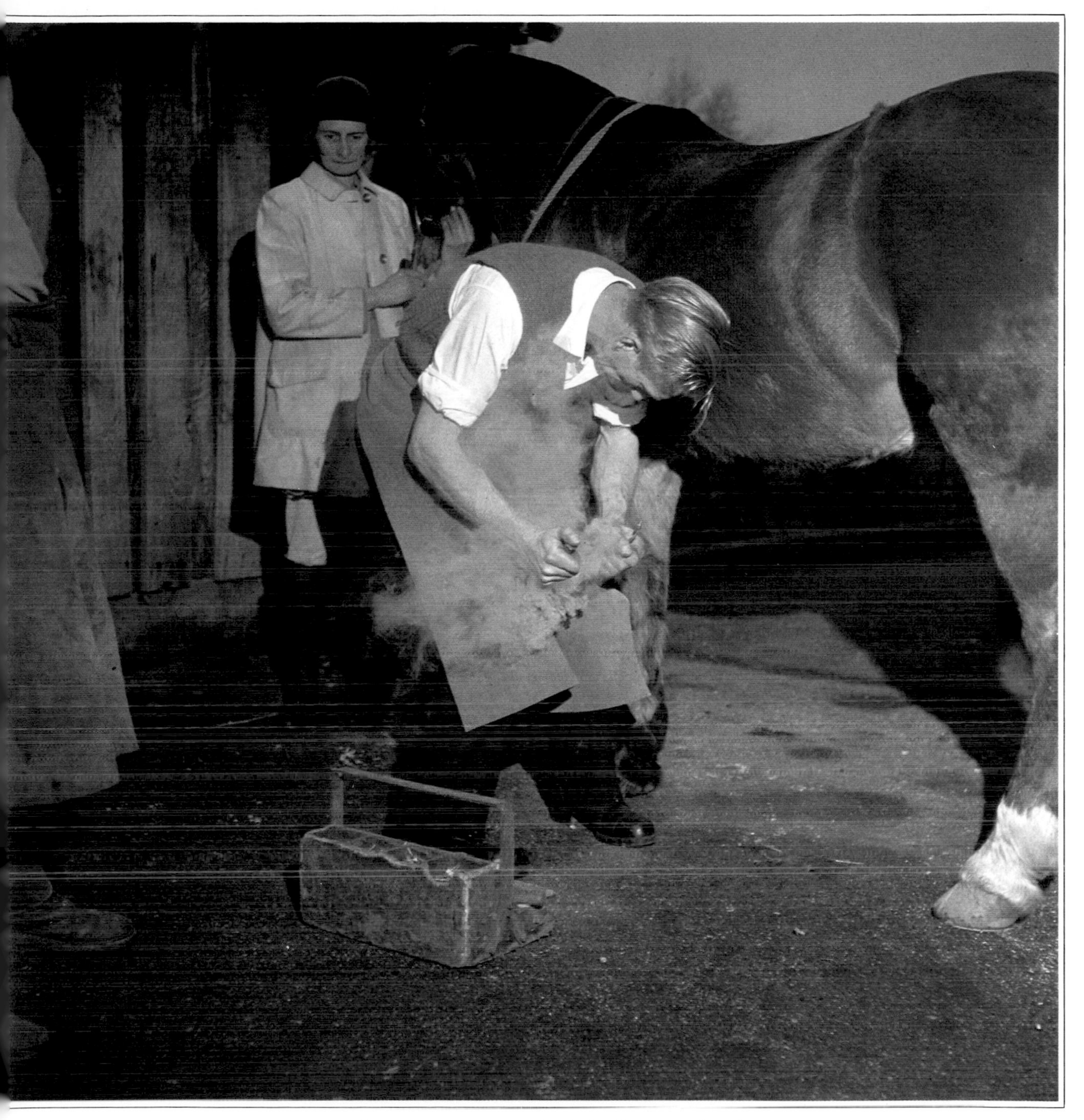

Until the advent of the motor car, the blacksmith was a key figure in any rural community. The forge was just as much a meeting-place as the pub for the exchange of farming gossip, while the shoeing of a fractious horse could be splendid entertainment — for the onlookers.

The fox, beautiful and intelligent creature that it is, seems to arouse, more than any other quarry, the excitement and blood-lust of hunting-men. The legendary John Peel even sold off some of his land to support the hunt and on the very day his son died he rushed off after a fox that had been 'viewed'.

In the early days of compulsory education, 'mitching' or truancy was rife among country children. At one village school with fifty children on its register, between 1875 and 1892 the weekly attendances never exceeded twenty-nine and fell as low as eleven.

There are few village schools nowadays with an attendance of forty-five, as in Flora Thompson's *Lark Rise*. Many of those children had to walk several miles, setting off after a seven o'clock breakfast. Today, the daily school bus to the town drains away the life of the village.

MARCH

'Good turn out, eh?' murmured the Brigadier, as we shuffled out of our little church and followed the bearers and the mourners and the congregation into the graveyard at Mrs Dunch's funeral. 'She really was part of the village. D'you know, I can remember, when I was a boy and used to come and stay with my uncle, old Dunch dying, the grandfather, that's to say. There was only a rough track to their cottage — thatch and cob, well, it still is — cob's all right so long as the rain doesn't get in it — and they had to carry the coffin across the fields as far as the Drover's Road and there there was a horse and cart waiting for them.'

Yes, I thought, and I too can remember when the Dunches had a milkround. That's an echo from the past in these days when, officially at least, you cannot buy a drop of milk from any farm in the village — it all has to be sent by bulk-tanker thirty miles away, and then comes back, bottled, to be delivered on your doorstep, not even by a villager, but by the dairyman from Fleckham.

For many years, too, old Dunch used to take passengers to and from the station in the market-town in his pony and trap. This was gradually superseded by Farley the blacksmith who invested in a motorcar. That caused great acrimony for a long time, and if Farley found himself driving behind Dunch, he was obliged, until he reached the main road, to putter along at the same speed as the horse, for Dunch was doggedly impervious to all the indignant hooting that went on.

To Cushy Doe's unspoken relief, Mrs Dunch had hung on until more clement times, for Cushy is a real old-fashioned sexton. Unlike most of his *confrères* in other parishes who merely tend the church stove or cut the grass or put out the hymn-books, he actually digs the graves, instead of this being contracted for by the undertaker. And he does so with remarkable skill, cutting the deep sides with machine-like neatness so that you can easily believe 'the houses that he makes last till doomsday'.

Almost more remarkable is the fact that he still contrives to find room for yet more sleepers to be tucked away in those grassy slopes, where the first primroses are now taking the place of the snowdrops. After all the countless generations that have been buried there, you would have expected him to need the equivalent of a theatre-booking chart where all the reservations are filled in — although it has to be said that the Parish Council has its eye on an adjoining paddock in the corner by Church Cottages. The owners are not keen to sell and there are vague mutterings about compulsory purchase, which would have to be effected by the District Council on behalf of the parish, which does not have the powers. We have no recreation ground, but room must be made for the dead.

'Forasmuch as it hath pleased Almighty God of his great mercy to take unto himself the soul of our dear sister here departed, we therefore commit her body to the ground; earth to earth, ashes to ashes, dust to dust . . . '

Mrs Dunch's grand-daughter casts a posy of Lent lilies into the grave (it is nearly Easter, and the church is tenderly brilliant with masses of them gathered in the meadows by the river). The old lady's sons, themselves middle-aged, thickset, deliberate men, massively shapeless from a life of physical toil, and encased in that rigorous stiff black all country people possess, cast earth upon the coffin. And as the Rector, imposing in his voluminous black cloak, lined with red, recites the committal, I glance round the villagers — heedless of the soft spring rain that seems almost green with the promise of the growth it will encourage — assembled there with demurely bowed heads and folded hands, and surrounded by all the grey headstones which somehow, fancifully, have suddenly become more prominent, as if the sleepers underneath them were aware of this addition to their numbers and were watching intently to find out who it was.

It had been a good turn-out, and the Brigadier hadn't been facetious. You only go to a wedding or a christening if you are invited, but at a village funeral 'everybody' attends — either because of the dead person or out of respect and sympathy for the family. There is a definite protocol in village life which shows up at funerals. Joy is self-supporting and needs no reassurance; but even those who don't ordinarily go to church turn out for a funeral. Unless you are the most hard-boiled materialist, there is still that mysterious, darkling, unbelievable finality about it all. Death has got its sting, whatever the prayerbook says. And both actually and metaphorically, we are staring over the brink and trying to fathom it out as we watch the coffin being lowered on its ropes into that wormy abyss. We would agree with Masefield that 'death opens unknown doors', but not necessarily that 'it is most grand to die'.

At the same time there is an immutable peace about a country graveyard, in contrast with the awful, clinical, convenience-packaging, impersonality of the crematorium, with that ghastly piped music, the feeling that the priest-in-residence is doing it all by rote, and the dead person in the coffin sliding away out of sight like luggage on a conveyor belt at an airport, to be consumed in oil-fired furnaces, rather than mingling with the everlasting earth. Every hyacinth springing from some once lovely head may be a sentimental and unlikely platitude, but at least it's better than those left-over bones that just don't get processed.

The church tower glows with patches of golden lichen that spread over its granite. The stained-glass windows gleam, bringing to life St Joseph at his carpenter's bench. Watchful by the lych-gate our solitary yew stands, massively dark and brooding, its red and clustered columns as much witnesses of a thousand such burials as the columns in the church itself. Wordsworth might have had our yew tree in mind when he wrote :

> Of vast circumference and gloom profound
> This solitary tree! — a living thing
> Produced too slowly ever to decay;
> Of form and aspect too magnificent
> To be destroyed. A pillared shade
> Upon whose grassless floor of red-brown hue,
> By sheddings from the pining umbrage tinged
> Perennially — beneath whose sable roof
> Of boughs, as if for festal purpose decked
> With unrejoicing berries — ghostly shapes
> May meet at noontide; Fear and trembling Hope,
> Silence and Foresight; Death the Skeleton;
> And Time the Shadow —

And in the mauve-hazed elms (so far spared that strangled death which has afflicted so many of the species), the rooks, heedless of man's affairs, are busy repairing their nests, but their persistent cawing is as natural and unobtrusive as the notes of the first chiff-chaff in the Town Farm hedge or the lowing of a cow — while in tender irony, so apt it might almost be contrived, as the Rector forecasts the changing of Mrs Dunch's vile body so that it shall be like the glorious body of the Lord Jesus Christ, there comes from farther down the village the sound of children playing in their afternoon break.

There has been a good turn-out for Mrs Dunch's departure, and there will be again at Easter, when shining faces and ecstatic if erratically pitched voices express a new-found fervour that will last at least until Sunday dinner-time.

Normally, however, the church is rarely more than half full, and Cushy Doe once swore in the pub that you could tell where the regulars sat because the oak pews are so polished in certain spots.

We may even attract a larger congregation than some neighbouring parishes do, for ours is a pleasant church to worship in, with its graceful arcades which impart to it a deceptive impression of spaciousness, for it is in fact not really big, while the light that filters down through some of the stained glass is at times of a dreamlike dove-rosiness, exactly the tinge on a ring-dove's feathers. In addition, the carved bosses of the roof and the rood-screen which escaped the attention of Victorian restorers are, as the guide-books say, worthy of note. But for me, at least, the most interesting feature is the gallery — memory of the days when in country churches villagers provided the music instead of an organ or harmonium, as in Hardy's *The Return of the Native*:

> 'Twas the Hundred-and-thirty-third to 'Lydia' — and when they'd come to 'Ran down his beard and o'er his robes its costly moisture shed', Neighbour Yeobright, who had just warmed to his work, drove his bow into them strings that glorious grand that he e'en a'most sawed the bass-viol into two pieces. Every winder in church rattled as if 'twere a thunderstorm.

Apart from the charm of this partly fourteenth-century building, some people go to church because of the Rector; and at the same time other villagers who never attend church respect the Rector not for his cloth but because of his character. Unlike some priests who are only concerned with the faithful, our Rector regards all the parishioners as his responsibility (ninety and nine just persons there may be, but you never know when that one sinner may repent). When such an unpromising candidate as Alf Whittle, the lorry-driver, renowned for his picturesque and violent blaspheming, had a bad accident, the Rector travelled a hundred miles there and back to visit him in the hospital where he had landed up. And he is always prepared to engage in an argument with the deepest dyed atheist, although it has to be admitted that certain political names tend to make his wattles colour up somewhat. Besides, he does not restrict his parish activities to ecclesiastical ones. He is often to be seen flighting a skilful dart in The Lamb, while we are proud of the fact that he has earned his place as an opening batsman in the village cricket team through sheer merit and not because Reg Dredge, captain of the bell-ringers is also captain of the cricket club.

But if we are fortunate in our parson, it has to be admitted that the church's influence in the countryside in general has steadily waned during many generations. In our village there is a core of faithful, some such as the Brigadier reckoning it is like a parade which you just have got to attend, while there is a devoted posse of ladies who take it in turn to arrange the flowers. Others are still like Flora Thompson's villagers, half of whom went to church to show off their best clothes and see and criticize those of their neighbours, and the other half because they loved to hear their own voices raised in hymns.

It is often imagined that one of the prime reasons for the church losing much of its influence was because of the revolution implicit in the theories of Charles Darwin and others. This of course was so, and fearful was the travail. But as far as the agricultural community was concerned, the church had already forfeited much of its influence and respect through the hated tithe system (for many centuries a compulsory tax, which caused great bitterness). Special tithe barns, often of magnificent character and proportions, were built to accommodate all the produce involved, for payment was in kind. 'The tenth sucking-pig went to the parson's table; the tenth sheaf was carried off for his benefit.' Only 150 years ago was this system commuted into a rent-charge and only in recent times was the system abolished. At times the greed of the parson was comic in its extremity.

In the past only the rich or well-to-do could afford monuments to their dead. Old, unmarked graves would be dug up and the bones deposited in crypt or charnel-house, to make room for new tenants. For many poor families who often had to share one bed, this 'move over' process was nothing new.

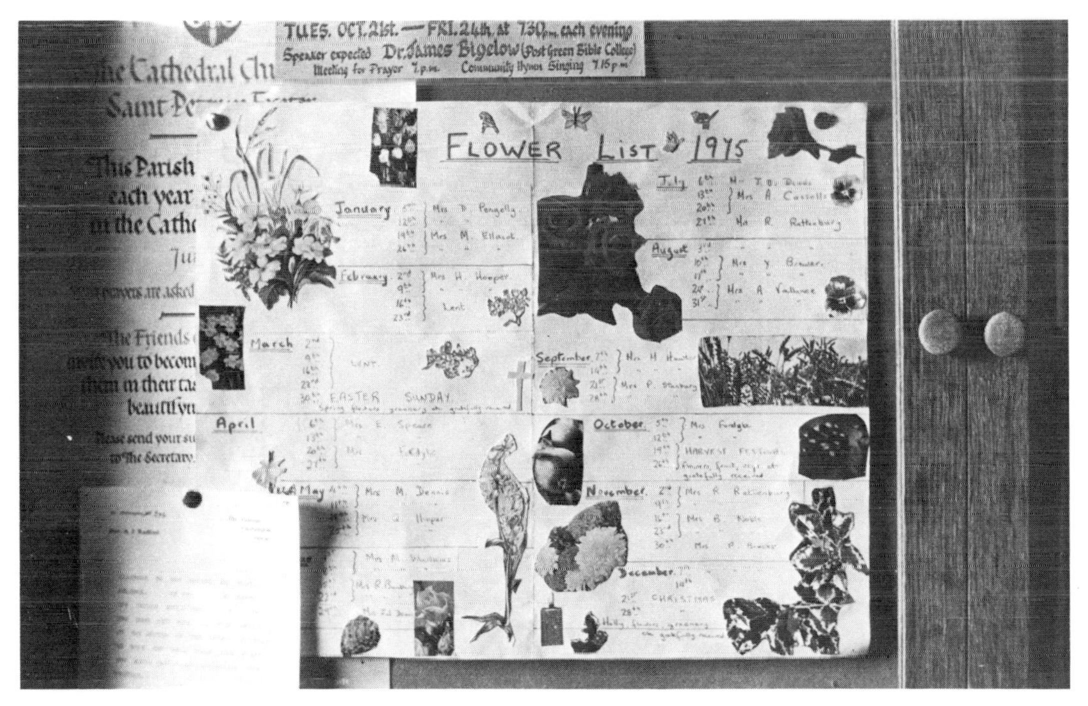

Decorating the church with offerings of flowers is an example of the adaptation of pagan customs into Christian traditions.

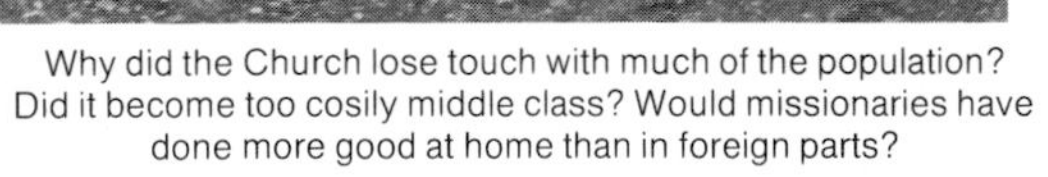

Why did the Church lose touch with much of the population? Did it become too cosily middle class? Would missionaries have done more good at home than in foreign parts?

This lychgate (lych means corpse) does not possess one, but in many cases there used to be a coffin-table on which the bearers rested their burden, maybe after a labouresome journey across the fields, while the priest recited part of the burial service. If the dead person were from a poor family, the body would be removed from the coffin and buried in a simple shroud — which at one time had by law to be made of wool, to encourage the wool-trade.

The country parson who can offer the rural community what it thirsts for will not be a sporting parson, not a games master, or an organizer of fantastic revels, but a thinker prepared to take his ideas out into the open and act upon them.

E.W. MARTIN, *The Secret People.*

'In choirs and places where they sing, here followeth the anthem.'

There was one famous case when a clergyman claimed a tithe upon the wild ducks that were being regularly trapped in a decoy. He lost his case because of the fact that the birds were wild, whereupon he claimed a tenth of the eggs laid by the farmyard ducks being used as decoys.

Traditionally, in a village community, the natural ally of the parson was the squire — or vice versa. The 'big house' was as important as the church; indeed, when the accompanying property was probably by far the largest in the parish, it was more important. Our big house is The Hall, a pleasant Georgian mansion (what Georgian dwelling is not pleasant; the style emphasizes the lost opportunities of modern architecture with its tooth-sucking monstrosities). The owner of The Hall is a retired surgeon, a fanatical bird-watcher, who, until the villagers became used to him, caused them moments of consternation by turning up in the most unexpected places, often on all fours and armed with camera. This was sometimes a hazardous occupation, particularly in the vicinity of Lover's Lane alias the Drover's Road, for some people, not unreasonably, prefer certain of their activities to be completely private.

But although he inherited The Hall and its acres from a distant relative, who once upon a time could genuinely have been called the squire, before most of the land was sold off, the present occupant has no aspiration to take an active leadership in village life. He is President of the Cricket Club, however, and gives it the use of a field, while his wife is President of the Women's Institute and has started a painting class — one of those nice Victorian activities that has been revived in recent years.

Well, this question of a squire — and by implication the leadership of a village — can be a vexed one. As for long-established 'residents' (as they are still distinguished even in these democratic days from the 'villagers'), such as the Brigadier and Captain RN, although both are active and often at loggerheads on, say, the Church Council over such matters as heating the church ('If Captain RN says that's the best way, it's bound to be wrong' — conversely 'The Brigadier thinks the sudden affluence of oil in the North Sea is due to an increase in the whale population'), neither is tactless enough to interfere unasked in village affairs.

Nor is a newcomer such as Mr Bragham. He is, as we have said, full of good works, but certainly is not obtrusive. Other newcomers tend to be too pushy, as in all villages, such as the retired property speculator who presides over the village hall as if it were the White House, or the cattle-dealer who throws pretentious barbecues ('Can't get rid of his meat, else,' they mutter in the pub), sends his children to a private school Squeers might have recognized, and now, latest badge of his social progress, keeps peacocks on his lawn. Such people would dearly have liked to be squire. As John Clare said:

> Young farmer Bigg of this same flimsy class
> Wise among fools and with the wise an ass
> A farming sprout with more then farmers pride
> Struts like the squire and dresses dignified
> They call him squire at which his weakness aimd
> But squires still view him as a fool misnamed

Now, squire and squirearchy are words almost as emotive as hunting.

Certainly not everyone would sing as in Dickens' *The Chimes*:

> Oh let us love our occupations,
> Bless the squire and his relations,
> Live upon our daily rations,
> And always know our proper stations.

And of course there were plenty of rural equivalents of Colonel Blimp, or 'uncouth, bucolic oafs', among the ranks of the squirearchy. Throughout the ages they have been caricatured — Shallow in *Henry IV*, Squire Western in Fielding's *Tom Jones*, Dr Johnson's Squire Bluster, Thackeray's Sir Pitt Crawley, who drank himself senseless every night, beat his wife, spoke in the coarsest and vulgarest Hampshire accent and was 'an old, stumpy, short, vulgar, and very dirty man, in old clothes and shabby old gaiters and cooks his own horrid supper in a saucepan'.

But to balance such horrors there was Joseph Addison's peerless Sir Roger de Coverley, that paragon of bumbling kindliness and good works, whose greatest tyranny was in church.

> As Sir Roger is landlord to the whole congregation, he keeps them in very good order, and will suffer nobody to sleep in it besides himself; for if by chance he has been surprised into a short nap at sermon, upon recovering out of it he stands up and looks about him, and if he sees anybody else nodding, either wakes them himself or sends his servant to them.

That of course sums it up! He was landlord to the whole congregation, so obviously enough could influence them. But there were squires in real life who not only contributed to the well-being of their own particular patch of England, but also nationally as well, especially, and naturally enough, in agricultural progress. In this respect, several eighteenth-century figures were all squires: Jethro Tull, who invented the corn-drill; Turnip Townsend who so revolutionized animal-feeding methods as to double the weight of cattle and sheep; Coke of Norfolk, whose farm at Holkham became an international showpiece to which even the Tsar of Russia sent a delegation to study methods (was that how Tolstoi's Levin got his advanced ideas?).

But in addition to his role as landlord and farmer in his own right, the squire performed many necessary functions in the life of the community. He acted as a Justice of the Peace, administered schools and friendly societies and other institutions, saw to the proper functioning of the Poor Law, and was almost always interested in the well-being of the workhouse. Some people, of course, would suggest that the squirearchy contributed to that same poverty which existed. W.H. Hudson certainly thought so and couldn't stand the squire, detesting the effect of his position on the inferior minds around him, and the servility, hypocrisy, and parasitism which flourished in his wide shadow.

Well, all this doesn't obtain with us, for we have a squire in name only. But occasionally, when the village has one of its silly fits, I think of the words of John Scott two hundred years ago: 'Happy is the parish that has got a good King.'

If the influence of parson and squire is a shadow of what it was, who would qualify as king of the parish? Who runs the village? Latterly I've wondered a lot about this. Now, on Church Green, the side nearest the cottages, where the road narrows, there stands the village pump. For long generations many of the villagers, especially in the main cluster of dwellings, depended on this, and it must have been hard work humping pails of water to and fro. It is surprising, however, what an immense difference a yoke makes — you can carry buckets literally full to the brim without spilling a drop, while the yoke distributes the burden more evenly, instead of the arms being stretched painfully as if on a rack.

And up to about eighteen years ago or less, Sam Dredge, whose tiny cottage is directly opposite the pump, used frequently to conduct his morning ablutions at the pump. He would carefully place his false teeth on a ledge by the entrance to the pump and they would grin out at any passerby as if on guard while their owner sluiced away.

The pump itself was erected nearly 150 years ago, according to the maker's plaque, although undoubtedly one existed there beforehand. Then, some years later, an unknown benefactor — even Sam, our unofficial archivist, cannot put a name to him or her — erected a little lead-roofed 'pavilion' over the pump, so that people could gossip happily, sheltered from the weather, while waiting their turn. In addition, a cattle-trough was added, for at that time the farm animals wandered about the place as freely as sacred cows in a Hindu market.

Once main water was laid on, the familiar scruppeting of the pump handle fell silent, the pump and its shelter became part of the scenery, to be photographed by summer visitors, while some people occasionally turn up to wash their cars at it, and Mr Slocum's ducks dabble in the deliciously muddy overflow which spills across the road.

Recently, however, this relic of the past was brought abruptly to our attention again. Alf Whittle, who, to the complaints of many, often parks his lorry on the edge of the green, ravaging the grass and polluting the place with noise and stink, backed into the side of the shelter, damaging it considerably.

Immediately the village divided into factions, pro-pump and anti-pump. Useless, take it down, it's an anachronism, taking it away would make more room for cars as they come round the corner from Market Lane. Alf Whittle and Mr Counter, the ex-bank manager, who lives in one of the tarted-up cottages, join forces in their agitation for the removal of the pump and its little house. As far as Alf is concerned, it is a question of attack being the best form of defence, for he knows he is highly unpopular with his ugly great six-wheeler. And Mrs Counter, used to the primness of Crassville, frequently complains about the permanent eddy of mud that threatens her front door.

All this is met by an even sturdier and more numerous opposition, led by Captain RN. It would be scandalous if the pump were done away with. It's symbolic of the past and a reminder that life was not always cosily picturesque in the countryside — no drains, a scratch-box at the bottom of the garden, and every single drop of water having to be brought to the kitchen by hand — except for the fortunates who had a well in their garden or backyard.

The gallant Captain descended like a force ten gale on the chairman of the Parish Council, Mr Deedes, the Fleckham lawyer. 'Repair the sides of the shelter, brick walls round three sides and on the green side you could convert the drinking-trough into a seat. Marvellous view from there, with The Lamb and the church and the shop and the timbered cottages, and Rooky Wood in the background.' He brushed aside objections that the pump and its shelter would still be liable to damage by careless vehicles. 'That's the point, don't you see, man — now's your chance! Protect the village green! You've talked about it long enough — it was brought up at last year's parish meeting. It's a crying shame the way cars — especially that damned lorry — are allowed to churn it up. It's being eroded, visibly. Post and chains are what you want —'

'We don't know the legal position! There's no record of who put the thing up! Besides, the expense . . .'

'What's the Parish Council for, for God's sake, man! As to the cost, you can raise a penny rate, you know that! That brings in around £400 here! And look — if you're thinking of going in for the Best-kept Village competition next year, this would clinch the matter!'

It was this prospect that raised a gleam in the lawyer's neutral eye, for to enter the Best-kept Village competition was a matter dear to his worthy heart. The poor fellow often wondered why he bothered to continue as chairman, there was so little the Parish Council could do. Half the village could not have named the seven members of the Council — they weren't even elected, but were invariably returned unopposed, partly through indifference, partly to save the village electoral expenses.

'If you care to make a submission to the Parish Council, Captain — '

'Dammee, man, make a submission?' snorted Captain RN. 'Oh, you mean, write a letter? I certainly will — and I'll get you fifty signatures at the drop of a hat!'

So, we live in hope that this relic of past village life — the pump, I mean — will be saved, and also that our village green will at last be protected from the insidious four-wheeled invasion that has crept on apace these many years. Perhaps, impelled by Captain RN, the Parish Council will act, in so far as it can, for it is ironical that the modern parish council (created by an Act of 1894) has far less effective power than the old 'vestry'. This was closely connected with the church and enjoyed extensive local powers, even though it was far from democratic, being composed of the more affluent members of the community. But the churchwarden, for example, was an important executive, one might say, while the parish constable was sometimes greatly feared, having the right to arrest offenders and consign them to the village lock-up, while the stocks, whipping-post, and ducking-stool were all in his charge.

So, the power and influence of all three — parson, squire, parish council — have faded into virtual nothingness. Whatever their faults, prejudices, injustices, they were at least more intimate than the faceless men of District Council and County Council.

APRIL

The point-to-point is the grand climax of the fox-hunting season. Even those who are not devotees of hunting itself go to the races. In the village we are lucky because the local hunt's point-to-point is held within walking distance — at least for those energetically disposed — on a farm in one of the neighbouring parishes. It isn't every farmer who is so dead keen about the hunt that he relishes the idea of half a dozen races, involving heavy hunters, churning up hill and down dale across his land — in addition to which a couple of fields have to be turned over for the car-park and the spectators and the bookies and the tote and the first-aid tent and the weighing-in tent and the refreshment marquee and what not.

The farmer in question, however, Percy Shaddock of Otterholt, is far keener on the hunt and all its associated activities than he is on the science of agriculture. Walking hound-puppies, organizing the hunt ball, the hunt itself, and of course the point-to-point, Mr Shaddock is always in the van. He is one of those ferocious little men bedevilled by an abundance of energy that has to be continually alleviated by a sort of spiritual blood-letting, which, as far as the hunt is concerned, takes on a literal character, while to witness his reactions when a posse of hunt saboteurs once turned up was truly to believe that Dewer rode again!

So now, the energetic among us troop out of the village along the Drover's Road, which is becoming daily more thickly starred with primroses, while even the blackthorn lingers on — and, yes, it is — there goes a swallow, cleaving the air with metallic blue wings, almost doing a victory roll on returning to its native land; the chiff-chaff, of course, has long ago been heard. Brimstones flicker here and there like pallid shards of the sun, and faded tortoiseshells emerge from their winter sleep. The cuckoo is calling (it is difficult to understand that many people cannot bear that ineffable wandering voice), and the blackbirds only cease their mellow chorus of contentment when the hurrying feet draw near. All nature seems to be rejoicing that the hunting-season is over, and it is nice to think that as we stride on past the well-known Pyet Copse there is maybe a fox cocking an ear cautiously as it lies curled up in its earth.

Already we can see a long line of motorcars winking in the sun as they crawl over Starvation Hill, directed by George Huggins, the AA scout, while a flashing blue light shows that PC Keane (almost certainly it is he) is already on duty, for he knows that Black-eyed Susie will be there helping in the refreshment tent. We hurry on, afraid of missing any of the afternoon's activities; in the distance behind us the church clock is just striking two o'clock.

The point-to-point (and all of its more spectacular relations such as the Grand National and the Gold Cup) has its origins in the nefarious, notorious and often brutal steeplechase. Such racing is still so called, of course, but without the epithets which applied once upon a time, in the days of our great-great-great-grandfathers. The original steeplechase was just that: a tearaway cross-country run, regardless of whose property you were charging over, from one point to another, the most convenient and prominent being various parish church steeples or towers.

The critical adjectives used earlier were perfectly justified, for the steeplechase a century or two ago was a harsh affair as far as the horses were concerned. (Who was it who said that England was the paradise of women, the purgatory of men, and the hell of horses?) Nobody could have been a keener fox-hunter than R.S. Surtees, yet in *Mr Sponge's Sporting Tour* he lays aside his usual humorous detachment and urbanity to voice his condemnation of steeplechasing in uncompromising terms, depicting it as a veritable massacre. One horse is drowned, another breaks its back, a third is savagely cut to pieces by the overriding it is subjected to, while as for the riders, although that was their look-out, there were more injuries than most fox-hunters saw in a lifetime, and one of the more odious

An upgraded version of the Point to Point, the first Grand National was known as 'The Great Steeplechase' and was held in 1839. It was won by a horse named Lottery, ridden by James Mason.

characters gets killed, 'rolled up on the far side of a jump like a ball of worsted, with a broken neck'. But at least that particular grand aristocratic steeplechase ended in farce. The egregious Sponge who had, in the interests of a hoped-for betting coup, arranged to lose the race, was unable at the last moment to prevent his horse from bolting past the post, and, to the immense chagrin of himself and his collaborators, running out the winner.

Our point-to-point, however, is a less sordid affair than all that. For the village it is one of the most welcome outings of the year, both for its own sake and because it really marks the end of winter — besides, horses always excite the countryman even if he has never in his life set foot in the stirrups. So, long before the first race, Starvation Hill echoes with a thousand voices, louder than on any market-day. And, as at market-day, an almost tangible air of gusto pervades the scene. Just as appetite begets appetite, so too does noise beget noise. People seem almost to swell, they give the impression that they have become larger than when you last saw them in The Lamb or the village shop or walking down Market Lane, and their voices become louder accordingly. It is partly because they are enjoying themselves — and the human-being using his voice can be rather like a child playing on a toy-drum. You can get immense satisfaction at times using your vocal cords — and you don't have to sing. Perhaps, with Cowper, people feel that 'the noisy man is always in the right'.

To begin with, apart from what Fred Marks sardonically calls the shooting-stick brigade doing their little social performances around their cars (British 'warms' *de rigueur*), the crowd is divided into three or four main groups, each like a gigantic swarm of bees, and buzzing like one, too. The refreshment tent, from which wafts that inimitable beery effluvium, draws the biggest swarm — and much of it loyally clings to the Queen B all day. The paddock — which gives off that typical equine smell of ammonia from the staling horses who become quite as keyed up as their riders — draws a smaller but equally appreciative swarm. Its members vary from the tweedy connoisseur to the village family oohing and aahing at all the proud, glossy, sweating greys and blacks and bays and roans, and speculating on whether one of them might not be next year's winner of the Grand National — which isn't all that far-fetched. Many such winners have started their careers in a point-to-point race — was there not even one champion that had once pulled a milk-float?

In the meantime, the swarm around the beefburger vans has transferred much of its allegiance to the bookies' stands as Honest Joe Fleecer, who operates at all the best-known courses from Aintree to Cheltenham, or Sterling Will Cutpurse, who always gives the longest odds, are beginning to chalk up or shout the prices for the first race. And at the little rabbit-hutch of the tote a small man peers hopefully through his grille as a young boy comes up clutching a fifty-pence piece equally hopeful not only that he will win but that he won't be turned away as under-age.

And as the time for the first race draws close, the crowds begin to drift towards the finishing stretch, from which they can also see the start several undulating fields away. The riders make last-minute adjustments to girths and buckles and straps, the Clerk of the Scales rushes out with a weight-cloth for a belated entrant, the Clerk of the Course, bowler-hatted and encased in violent checks, strides out purposefully, armed with flag and loud-hailer, and the farmers' sons and the 'gentlemen farmers' (that peculiar breed of animal which likes to pretend it still exists long after it has become extinct) are given a leg-up. The saddles creak, and the horses, smelling the battle from afar, snort and scatter the gawking onlookers by lashing hoof or other equally drastic means.

Meanwhile, the knowledgeable have been walking the course, eyeing the country with expert appraisal and sizing up the jumps, in the hope that they will be taken for riders who are entered for a later race (the Open, of course) and who have not yet changed. And those who like to savour the essential atmosphere of the point-to-point do not return to see the finish. They stay out in the country alongside one of the worst jumps, red flag to the right, white on the left, perhaps in company with a couple of St John's Ambulance men.

It is there that the real drama takes place. You can also see the start from there, horses and riders appearing quite toylike in the distance of green fields, and stands of trees grouped like grave spectators bending over the scene. Away the riders go, disappearing for minutes on end at the bottom of Mr Shaddock's Grandacre and we wait tensely for their reappearance on the slopes of Hogget Ridge. Then the approaching thunder of hooves (without doubt one of the most terrifying, exciting, atavistically evocative sounds imaginable — God, to be faced by a cavalry charge must truly have turned your bowels to water!), the creaking of leather, champ of bit, the grunting and panting and all those other emphatic noises a striving horse makes, the flaring nostrils, the bulging eyes, the frothing mouths, the slimy flanks, the spattering gobbets of earth, and the riders in their striped and dotted and barred shirts crouching over their animals' withers. And then the momentary check, followed by one of the most astonishing physical feats ever performed — the huge, sixteen-hand horses, bearing riders of maybe twelve stone on their backs, taking off and clearing a five-foot hedge or bank of earth and stone, and landing at full stretch on the other side (especially clever are those riders who make for the gaps or holes torn in previous races). Some do not land at full stretch but in a fearful cartwheeling of massive body, thrashing

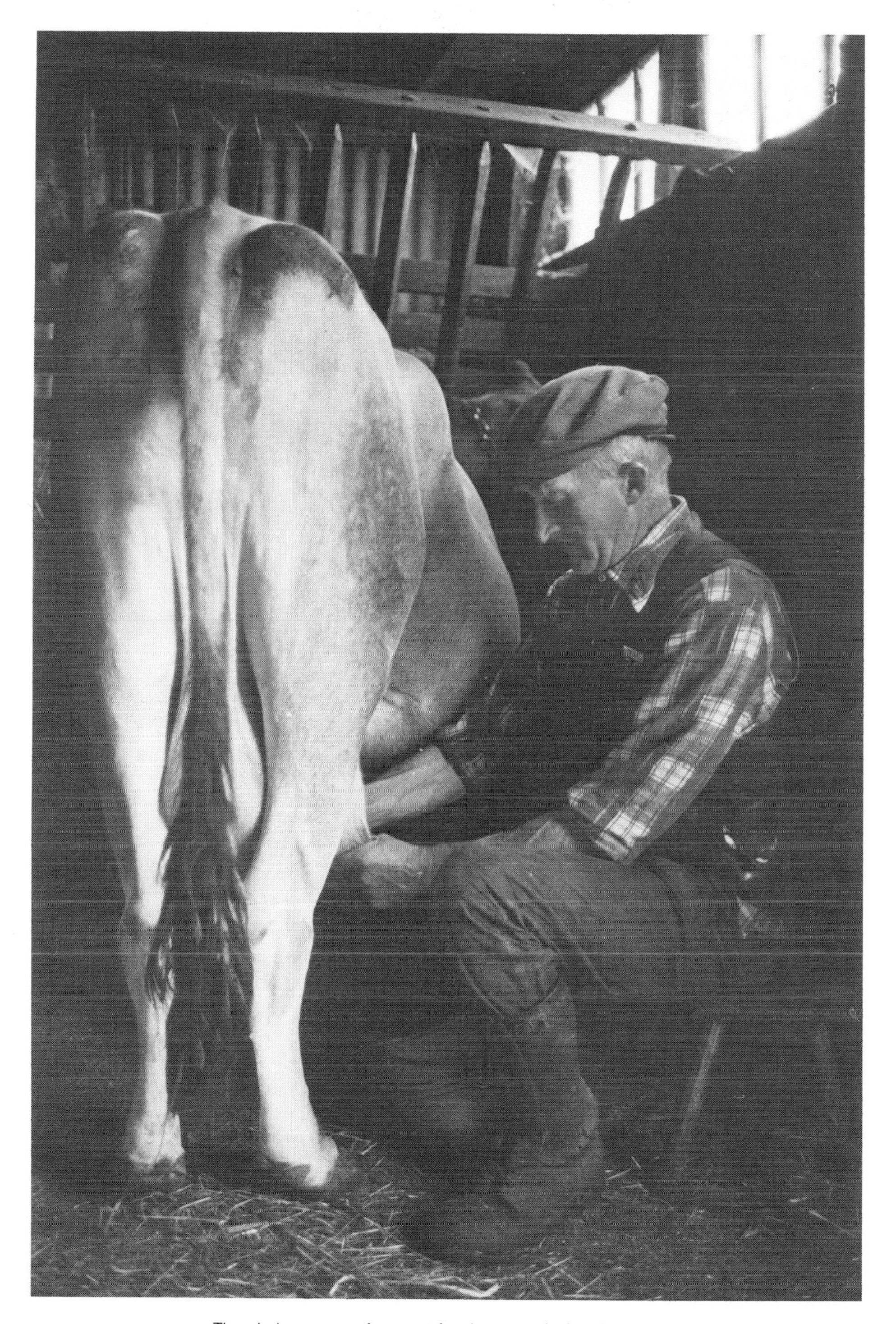

The whole process of peasant-farming, once the backbone of the country, becomes increasingly difficult:

Princes and lords may flourish, or may fade;
A breath can make them, as a breath has made;
But a bold peasantry, their country's pride,
When once destroyed, can never be supplied.

In Elizabethan times, Fynes Moryson wrote: 'A man cannot more freely command in his own house than he may do in his inn. And at parting, if he give some few pence to the chamberlain and ostler, they wish him a happy journey.'

He needed such a parting wish, for often the inn servants, even the landlord himself, were in league with local highwaymen, giving them useful information.

hooves, gay shirt, and, when the rest of the charge has faded across the field, the black and white uniforms rush out to succour the fallen, hopeful that nobody has suffered the fate of that unspeakable Jack Spraggon of Surtees' creation.

The Drover's Road, along which many of us trooped to the point-to-point, is a significant part of village history. First, however, we must mention the railway which passes across a segment of the parish boundary — or rather, alas, used to pass. It bisected meadows, pressed close against bluebell woods, flashed under secret bridges hardly ever seen on foot. Then the ground began to slope upwards and the train would plunge into a steep cutting, one side of which was in our parish, the other in Fleckham. The train would reappear fleetingly, as if it were checking its whereabouts, when little more than smoke and funnel and carriage-tops could be seen, then it would vanish into Broomball tunnel with an eldritch screech which unknowingly presaged the ultimate demise of the railway itself.

'Rain coming up tomorrow,' the locals would say. 'You could hear the old 4.20 as if her were chuffing down past church.'

The village never had a station of its own. There was one at Fleckham, while at Great Noshington, five miles away, certain trains stopped at the little halt. So the railway was of immense use to us, for going to the cathedral town, the market, and on rare occasions even up to London itself. And although it was a pleasure in daytime to pick out landmarks — Fleckham church-tower, Mrs Signalman's washing at the level-crossing on the main road, the quarry over 'to' Plasher Down, or individual flocks or herds — a night return was as exciting as ever it was in James Thompson's days 130 years ago:

> As we rush, as we rush in the train,
> The trees and the houses go wheeling back,
> But the starry heavens above the plain
> Come flying on our track.

Then the powers that be, ever more interested in cost effectiveness than in social amenities, began to run the rail service down. People in turn impatiently turned more and more to the motorcar, and, with cunning logic, the authorities then claimed that our line was no longer economically justified — no longer 'viable' was the word they used. 'Besides,' a certain minister remarked about rural transport in general, '*everybody* in the country has a motorcar nowadays.'

Everybody, that is, except our Cressie, Mrs Slee, Sam Dredge, Fred, Ken, Bill, Miss Flora Bundy, and all the rest and their counterparts countrywide. ('I took home sixty-eight quid this week,' says Fred. 'How can I run a car with four kids to bring up?') As far as the market-town is concerned there is a bus once a week. Otherwise, carless people have to rely on a lift from village motorists, of whom, of course, there is an ever-increasing number. At night and at weekends, the main street is lined with them, and the village green is being eroded away by them.

'Went to Finland for our holidays a few years ago,' says the Brigadier, pulling at his Guinness. 'Travelled all over the country in post buses. They take the mail and passengers all over the place. Why can't we do the same thing here, I ask you? Been talking about it long enough. No imagination, those desk-bound wallahs.'

So, all that remains of 'our' railway is a silent, empty, grassy track. The rails and the sleepers have been torn up, the little bridges pulled down. The only traffic along it nowadays is the occasional enterprising band of hikers (really walking, not hitching!) and the occasional fox, for Broomball cutting has become almost a nature reserve in its own right. A pair of kestrels nest in the brickwork of the tunnel entrance. Once or twice I have seen a barn owl float out of the depths, and heard its shriek, a mocking echo of the past. On the steepest part of the cutting, badgers are at work, their well-used latrines easily found. I only hope 'those most ancient of British beasts' will be safe from the renewed policy of gassing inaugurated by the men from the ministry supported by highfalutin enquiries whose scientific credibility has not been accepted by everyone. Among the floral jewels of the English countryside which grow there abundantly are gorse, bluebells, primroses, stitchwort, herb robert, periwinkles, pimpernel, yellow rattle, germander speedwell, and toadflax. The red and white campion must not be forgotten: 'Don't 'ee pluck neither of they,' warns Mrs Dredge. 'If 'ee plucks the red 'un, feyther'll die. Pick the whitey one and your poor mother will follow.' Dire advice indeed! It is best simply to stand and stare and wonder at all the galaxy of tiny jewels studding the turfy slopes.

Although the railway has vanished after perhaps 130 years, it is nicely ironical that another, far more ancient thoroughfare is still in use through part of the parish. This is the Drover's Road, as we still call it. As far as we are concerned, it starts in the far western corner of the parish at its junction with one of the main roads. It is a favourite walk, for in autumn it is festooned with old man's beard, gay with the pink berries of the guelder-rose and the hips of the wild rose, fiery with the leaves of the dogwood, while the hazel bushes hang out their clusters of nuts. In summer-time purple vetch climbs up the hawthorn, honeysuckle puts out its sweet-tasting little trumpets, trailing roses wander prodigally, far from their parent root, phalanxes of foxgloves stand in glorious array, and later in the ditches the heavy scented meadow-sweet thrusts up its frothy spikes. The wild birds seem aware of how all the riot of colour shows off their own colours. The yellow-hammers sit among the elderflowers, glorified by the sun. The goldfinch chooses the crab-apple. Green woodpeckers bound along showing off their brilliant yellow — popinjays, as Sam still calls them.

It is to Sam that I go to learn more about the Drover's Road. His father used to tell him how, as a boy, the drovers and their cattle and sheep, but cattle especially, would come regularly along the road and on through the village three or four times a year. For our generation, with its refrigerated lorries, cattle-trucks and deep-freezers in the home, it needs an effort of the imagination to visualize the difficulties of bygone days. In the country you were all but self-sufficient; but the towns, London above all, had to be fed by others..

All roads led to London, and through the year herds of cattle made the journeys of scores of miles across country, perforce on the hoof before the advent of railways and later refrigeration. Even turkeys used to go overland from East Anglia. Only the pig was spared such weary treks. He was mainly for home consumption, for pork kept less well than other meat, the rule being that one only ate pork with an 'r' in the month. Besides, the pig was not a willing pedestrian — although, in fact, Mary Mitford does mention him:

> That apparently lonely and trackless common is the very high road of the drovers who came from different parts of the West to the great mart, London. Seldom would that Green be found without a flock of Welch sheep, footsore and weary, and yet tempted into grazing by the short fine grass dispersed over its surface, or a drove of gaunt Irish pigs, sleeping in a corner, or a score of Devonshire cows straggling in all directions, picking the long grass from the surrounding ditches; whilst dog and man, shepherd and drover, might be seen basking in the sun.

His baite the least red worme that may be found
And at the bottome it doth always lye;
Whereat the greedy Goodgion bites so sound,
That Hooke and all he swalloweth by and by

JOHN DENNYS, 1613

And old Jorrocks, when he was living at Hillingdon Hall, used often to ride along one of these droves where:

> scarce a cart-rut broke its even surface, and its verdure was kept so close nipped by the cattle. The woodbine-entwined and rose-bending bushes of the high hedges in the narrow parts formed a cool shade, while broader places, widening into patches of common towards the hill-tops (over which these roads often pass), furnished cheap pasture for the loitering cattle. And along this drove, Mr Jorrocks encountered a large herd of Scotch kyloes [those fearsome-looking, shaggy, long horned Highland cattle], picking their way as they went. There might be fifty or sixty of them, duns, browns, mottles, reds and blacks, with wildness depicted in the prominent eyes of their broad faces.

By Napoleonic times, a hundred thousand head of cattle and three quarters of a million sheep were slaughtered annually in Smithfield market. (The arrival there of those shambling, panic-stricken herds was graphically described by Dickens in *Oliver Twist.*) And all those teeming mobs had travelled on the hoof along the spider-web of droves and so-called roads of which ours was a single thread.

For Sam's father the coming of the drovers was an exciting time, a welcome diversion from swinging his bird-scaring rattle or humping water from the village pump. He and other children would rush out along the drove to watch from some safe vantage-point the lowing, jostling, horn-tossing cattle — them especially, for they were more exciting than the sheep.

An echo of his excitement is to be found in George Bourne's Farmer Smith. At their village school, the boys used to enjoy their punishment of being made to stand on a bench when they could watch the drovers going past with their herds.

The droves numbered up to a hundred and fifty each and during the 'season' they would be passing continuously. With every herd there were four or five drovers on horseback, sometimes one riding pillion. And all along the main roads there were favourite inns, where a clever landlady was needed to satisfy those welcome guests and a skilful cook to keep the frying-pan in constant action, for fried liver and bacon was their staple diet.

The legions of livestock had to be catered for, too. Ten miles was an average distance each day, so a great deal of grazing was needed. 'All these arrangements clearly had to be planned out in advance; and if it was profitable to the farmers to sell their feed, the drovers for their part were shrewd at bargaining. Upright men, but close-fisted.'

Apart from the private grazing that might have been found down our way, one stretch of pasture the drovers used is still known as the Drover's Lea, a sixteen-acre piece of common on the outskirts of the village, where they harboured their animals for the night. A pond, still in existence, added to the amenities. 'One of the drovers, perhaps the owner of the stock, would ride three or four days in advance of his herd, buying up the feed; or sometimes he fell behind, to sell again for some other herd a piece of feed his own animals after all had not needed.'

In addition to the difficulties and hardships these overland treks must have involved, there were, far enough back in time, unexpected hazards. Highwaymen sometimes practised a protection racket at the expense of the drovers. One of the most notorious was William Nevinson, who, in return for a quarterly tribute, 'protected' the cattle-drovers from other highwaymen. He disliked competition and, on one occasion having encountered a party of drovers who had just been robbed by another gang, rode off, caught up with his rivals, forced them to hand over their booty and returned it to the drovers.

Although our railway has gone the Drover's Road is still in use, not simply as a Lover's Lane, but as a cattle thoroughfare (not as extensively as in olden times, however). George Hussey, who has a property in Fleckham as well as his farm near the village, uses the drove to transfer his cattle from one place to the other. And Russell of Frog's Bottom, when he is sending cattle off to market, finds it more practical for the animals to be brought along the drove and rendezvous with the truck in the village, rather than for the vehicle to risk his very steep hill.

So, although not even a ghost train goes bustling through Broomball cutting nowadays, at least along the drove you can sometimes see and hear a very tangible reminder of former days as the shambling, smooth-flanked red cattle make their way, snatching a mouthful of grass as they go. We have a fine church, stocks on the green, an ancient erstwhile coaching inn, but our Drover's Road (and those other green tracks which still exist in parts of the land) is just as much a part of English history as they are. To walk along it is truly to be near the throbbing heart of the countryside. Even in the early years of the nineteenth century William Cobbett observed that 'those who travel on turnpike roads [i.e. main roads] know nothing of England. In any sort of carriage you cannot get into the *real country places*.'

MAY

George Thornback is selling up. He farms Langtree on the northern edge of the parish, what might be called a traditional farm with a little of everything — a dozen milking cows, a hundred or so ewes, poultry, pigs, and of course an apple-orchard (the produce of which is always delivered to Mr Slocum). By modern standards Langtree is a small farm of only about ninety acres. But George *owns* it, as he was once heard to point out when being patronized by a larger tenant-farmer in the market. What he actually said was, 'The dirt on thiccy boots of mine belong to me and nobody else. My only landlord is the Lord a'mighty.'

George rarely came into the village during summer-time, for like all farmers he was too busy. In winter, however, he came regularly every Friday for a modest 'glass of ale', as he called it, for he drank little and always attended the Methodist Chapel at Furzedown Cross. His great passion was skittles and, as he put it, 'I like to hear 'em rumble-rumble down the alley, 'tis like tu the thunder of the A'mighty and he sends them ninepins a'clatterin' down!' And although he himself drank sparingly, he was never backward in carrying the can (which incidentally is the origin of the expression), in this case, an enormous enamel jug which had frequently to be taken across the courtyard of The Lamb to be replenished, especially when a visiting skittle-team was being entertained. There has probably been a skittle alley at The Lamb for centuries, and in recent years the game has everywhere been making a great come-back, although it does not yet rival that comparative upstart, darts.

George was the epitome of the yeoman farmer, the latter being described in *The Shorter Oxford English Dictionary* as 'a man owning and cultivating a small estate; a freeholder below the rank of gentleman; loosely a countryman of respectable standing'. George was certainly the latter. And again, as G.M. Trevelyan puts it: 'The praise of the yeoman as the best type of Englishman, holding society together, neither cringing to the high nor despising his poor neighbour, hearty, hospitable, fearless, supplies a constant motif of literature under Tudors and Stuarts. And it corresponds to a social fact.' But alas! the Thornbacks of this world are sparser on the ground these days.

I am not surprised that George is giving up. Walking across the furrows has tested him increasingly, and he has never been the same man since his wife died a year or two ago. (When she was alive, they were, as someone put it, like two rosy red pippins on the same twig.) And not long afterwards his youngest daughter got married, while John Pigeon, George's old hand, had to retire through arthritis. George has no son to take over from him, although his daughters and sons-in-law came over to help him out as often as they could, and he is going to live with them alternately.

The farm is being auctioned separately at the White Hart in Fleckham, but the sale of the livestock and deadstock was at Langtree itself. (When I was a boy it took me a long time to realize that deadstock referred to the farm implements and machinery, not to slaughtered animals!) The sale of anyone's home is by implication sad, but a farm sale is the most poignant of all. An entire way of life is entailed, and it isn't simply the farmhouse that is passing into other hands. It is the fields that have faithfully produced crop after crop, red wheat or delicate oats or fat golden swedes; the meadows brilliant now with the buttercups that George always swore made the cream; the little copses, where wood-pigeons cooed their praises of any kind of brassica or clover or turnip-tops; the rambling, thickset hedges where the yellow hammers are pointing out their liking for bread without cheese. All the familiar undulating landscape patched in so many colours has been known, every square yard of it, to George over forty years and viewed with pride and affection when, without fail, he would walk around it all of a Sunday — that nice old-fashioned farming custom, although you could not do it on some of the modern inflated agricultural properties.

And of course the animals are a part of that way of life, too. The ewes — close-wools crossed with Leicesters — would be solemnly marched by George up and down one particular lane twice a day for a fortnight before lambing-time, convinced that this forced promenade was good for their health when the lambs were heavy within them. Then there were the geese which, like grenadiers, would make George's sheepdog Fetch redundant, with their gaggling hullabaloo at the approach of any visitor. The ducks, which were sometimes followed by fluffy, toylike, whispering young ones, paddled bright-eyed on the little pond over which leaned perhaps the only quince-tree in the county. The cockerel, whose blood-red comb contrasts so vividly with its snow-white plumage, crowed to its hens from the eminence of the muck-heap, while the strange, furtively creeping guinea-fowl set up their jungle-racket of 'Go-back! Go-back!' as they went to roost in the apple-trees. The pigs which grubbed in the orchard, revelled in the mud or squealed piteously but unconvincingly that they were being starved to death, now, on the day of the sale, were lying cosily and deeply in yellow straw.

Above all, farm life was the cows. No pedigree herd this, with a smart little sign swinging over the farm-gate, but honest-to-goodness 'reds' and shorthorns which gave a modest thousand gallons a year. It was the sale of these cows that hit George the hardest. Ten thousand and one times he had called them in, 'Coop! coop! coop! Cush! cush! cush! Come along den!' — milking them twice a day, calving them down, selling off, buying in. Now, expressionless, he drove them, one at a time, around the yard in front of the audience — for audience it truly was, at least half the folk at any sale having not the slightest intention of buying anything — while the auctioneer kept up his verbal acrobatics.

Much later, when everything was over, I caught a glimpse of what it all meant to the old man. A cattle-lorry had come grinding into Langtree to fetch away some of the animals that had been purchased. George was helping to persuade them up the ramp. Out of the shippon ambled Daisy, a fine, sleek, swag-uddered red, which I knew to be his favourite. Uncertain what was expected of her, she hesitated, whereupon George dealt her a violent blow with his stick, and swore to boot. Never before had I known him belabour an animal like that and certainly not to swear. Bewildered at such an uncharacteristic assault, Daisy gazed around momentarily with huge, dewy, reproachful eyes, before stumbling on up the ramp, urged on by the lorry-driver and his mate. I happened to catch George's eye at that moment and we both looked away hurriedly.

'Dratted beast,' George mumbled defensively and, turning on his heel, took refuge in the gloom of the shippon, while nesting swallows flickered to and fro.

In *The Woodlanders* Thomas Hardy describes Marty South working at night by the light of the fire to help make a few pence to keep herself and her ailing father, whose job she has taken over:

> With a bill-hook in one hand and a leather glove much too large for her on the other, she was making spars, such as are used by thatchers, with great rapidity. She wore a leather apron for this purpose, which was also much too large for her figure. On her left hand lay a bundle of the straight, smooth hazel rods called spar-gads — the raw material of her manufacture; on her right a heap of chips and ends — the refuse — with which the fire was maintained; in front a pile of the finished articles. To produce them she took up each gad, looked critically at it from end to end, cut it to length, split it into four, and sharpened each of the

W H. Hudson's Caleb Bawcombe. 'I've been told shepherding's a poor way to spend a life, working seven days a week for thirteen shillings. But I never seen it like that; and I always did my best. You see, sir, I took a pride in it. I like my work and I liked knowing things about sheep. Not things in books, for I never had no books, but what I found out with my own sense, if you can understand me.'

quarters with dexterous blows, which brought it to a triangular point resembling that of a bayonet.

Reg Dredge the thatcher has certainly never read Hardy, but he would fully appreciate the work Marty was doing, for Reg's trade or craft has altered little through the generations. Indeed, almost more than any other, it is a skill passed on from generation to generation, and Phil, Reg's eldest son, is a case in point. When he left school he was unable to find any other work, so, logically, although Reg had hoped for 'better things' for him, Phil is now his assistant. Among other 'prentice chores, Phil does the work Marty was toiling at: the spars (so called in the West; spicks in Wiltshire; buckles in Worcestershire, and sprays in Buckinghamshire) are used for fixing the straw or reeds to the laths that run across the rafters.

Reg himself returned to the trade just in time to carry on the tradition from his father. When he left the Army he could have had any number of jobs, but all would have been far away from the village, and after a hectic six years' military service, including Dunkirk and D-day, he reckoned he wanted no more roaming, especially as, comparatively late in life, he had married a local girl.

For some years thatchers had a pretty thin time. Thatch was old-fashioned, a liability, a refuge for rats and sparrows, and insurance far more expensive than for a conventional dwelling. Many a cottage had its greening roof stripped off and slates or tiles substituted — although, in fact, well-made thatch will last for half a century and more. But, during the last fifteen years or so, there has been a boom in thatching. Made possible by the motorcar and desirable by the increasingly nerve-racking life of the town, the flight to the country — by those fortunate enough to be able to join it — gathered momentum. Once-dilapidated cottages were tarted up and the people who couldn't exist without a deep-freeze, dishwasher, central heating and a couple of cars, desired, at least superficially, nothing so much as an olde worlde appearance to their residence. Little did they realize what conditions in those country dream-cottages had been like in the past.

So, good luck to them. The thatchers flourished again, among them Reg, now master-thatcher, and he and his kind are relics of the days when the village community was a living organism and when, in return for their services to the community, the likes of the thatchers, the smiths, the carpenters, and all the other craftsmen were granted their arable strips, their portions of meadowland, home-closes, and pightles — those ancient paddocks for harbouring cattle at night.

You could say that the thatcher's skill, however primitive it was originally, stems farther back than that of those other craftsmen, for when man gave up living in caves and took to building his dwelling-huts, these had to be thatched, even if it was only with heather or turf-sods.

Although the motorcar, sacred cow of our era, has been responsible for the destruction or radical alteration of so many communities and traditional trades and crafts, yet, ironically, it has in some cases actually helped. As we have just seen, much of Reg's custom comes from those people who have fled to the country, their flight made practical by the motorcar; in addition, the motorcar (a little pick-up in Reg's case) enables him to travel long distances to work in other villages or towns where no thatcher exists. In olden times, horses and carts or Shank's pony restricted the sphere of the tradesman's work.

It was the same case for our village blacksmith. I can remember as a boy watching in awed fascination as Tom Farley worked in the smithy at the bottom of Four Post Hill. It was terrifyingly exciting, like some weird glimpse of hell, with the hammers ringing out (to be recognized in later years in that marvellous passage in Wagner's *Rheingold*, where the Nibelungs are at their work), the sullen flames brought to life by the bellows, the acrid smell as water was thrown on a red-hot shoe, the hissing fumes as the shoe was fitted on the sizzling hoof, and Tom himself, a dark-visaged hero scarcely heeding as his gigantic palm accidentally brushed the hell-hot iron. He was like that Ilmarinen in the Finnish *Kalevala* who was born at night-time, born upon a hill of charcoal, reared upon a plain of charcoal, in his hands a copper hammer and his little pincers.

When trade began to diminish Tom invested in a bull-nosed Morris Oxford and started a taxi-service, which, for a long time until cars became commonplace, was extremely useful for the village. Charley, Tom's eldest son, took over the taxi-service, installed a petrol pump, and gradually obtained more and more business, not merely in the village but from round about, being known as a willing and conscientious garagist, someone to be treasured. Having let the forge fall silent, the ageing Tom continued driving and then did his stint, a slightly lost soul, at the petrol pump. But Jack, the younger son, had iron in his veins, you might say. He went to a trade school and learnt the skill of iron-work, making handsome gates and even the holders for inn-signs. At that time, horse-riding was becoming popular again; of course, the hunt had always provided some work for blacksmiths, but the revival of horse-riding was among an entirely new section of the population, spear-headed by those jodhpured and velvet-capped small girls who have become a feature of the countryside. Most of them live in towns, but the motorcar, again, has made it possible for them to go out to the riding-schools and stables that have mushroomed everywhere. And so Jack Farley has profited from this, too. He has become a mobile smith, travelling far and wide in his van with his portable anvil and bellows.

Now, as a footnote to all that, I heard in The Lamb that a saddler has taken on our old baker's shop and is going to set up business there.

The following is another example of the ironical influence of the motorcar on village life.

The rowlocks creaked. The blades of the oars scattered showers of silver. Steadily Len Murren rowed out from the sandy shore of the river while his brother Frank stood in the stern of the boat, shooting the nigger-brown seine-net, one end of which was secured to the fishing-post in the bank, a gnarled round-shouldered birch, a pensioner of a tree that had done duty for generations. The lead-weighted net sank evenly as Frank paid out the meshes, then slowly it opened as the line of corks along the top floated to the surface. The seine settled like a fence in the shallow river, gradually enfolding in an unkind embrace any salmon that had lingered within the closing area.

Now Len was resting on one oar, rowing only with the other one to bring the boat round towards the shore to complete a half-moon. His hands working in unison, Frank continued to pay out the net until the very end. So exactly had Len judged the distance that the last meshes went over the stern as the little boat ground on the shore.

Frank clambered eagerly out into the water, clutching the ropes. He waded urgently in his rubber thigh-boots, fighting against the heavy meshes while the water swirled. Meanwhile, his brother dragged the boat out a little way among the tide-wrack, then went to his help. Together they hauled in the end of the seine-net a few paces so that there was no chance of any fish escaping. Once the 'leapers' knew that they were trapped they would thrash around desperately for a way out.

There are more than thirty breeds of sheep in Britain, all of them possessing individual qualities especially suited to their own region, but much profitable cross-breeding goes on which results in a large variety of wools.

Some lucky villages have been by-passed; others are victims of our failure to organize our lives better.

Many are the uses to which the osier has been put: muzzles for calves being weaned, carrier-baskets for pigeons, cradles for wine bottles, even the 'eel-grig', that ancient fish-trap.

The ropes secured, the men squatted down for a brief smoke while the rest of the team joined them, piratical in their thigh-boots and woollen caps. The haul itself would be a heavy job, even if there weren't many salmon, for the net was sodden. Every haul, however, was an eye-glinting gamble, for you never knew what there would be.

'There's one girt big 'un, master great fish, twenty pounder I woulden wonder. But not many more,' grunted Frank, balefully eyeing a heron majestically winging on its grey progress across the river, while a cormorant went speeding in the opposite direction, low above the pastel-shaded water.

'There's fewer fish in every darn year,' said another of the crew, taking his pipe from his mouth and spitting in a satisfying arc. ''Tis they Danish buggers off Greenland taking all the young smolts. All they Johnny-foreigners do use small meshes a bloody minnow couldn't get through.'

'I read in paper the other day,' someone else said, 'that they'm talking of restocking the rivers with Pacific salmon. Call 'em Coho salmon, they do!'

'Yoho, more like,' cried Frank, scrambling to his feet. 'Time to do a bit of heave-ho . . . '

Now, that scene did not take place in the village, but some twenty-five or thirty miles down-river, near the estuary. The point, however, is that Frank and Len have come to live in the village, in the council houses at Furzedown Cross, from which they run a small nursery and market garden, but they have for the time-being retained this share in a seine-netting franchise. At this time of year, amid a good deal of teasing hints about marital discord in the combined Murren households, they take themselves off to join their partners who are licensed to net a varying number of salmon each year. And they are one more example of the motorcar's influence in changing the human make-up of a village. It isn't only the Braghams of this world who have been able to find a different habitat: Alf Whittle, the lorry-driver, Mr Deedes, the Fleckham lawyer and young Maundy-Hansom, the architect, have all come to live in the village. Years ago, none of them would have been able to do so.

The eve of the brothers' departure down-river is marked by much chaffing and sarcasm on the part of the Brigadier and Captain RN, our two most enthusiastic fly-fishermen.

'I suppose there won't be another rise along our water for the rest of the season now,' grumbles the Brigadier, so tall he has to remember the ancient but unused brass oil-lamp (its gleaming brass, polished regularly by Mrs Dredge, does proxy for its light) swinging over the bar of The Lamb.

'Do you know, Brigadier,' Captain RN weighs in, 'that net fishermen take seven times the number of fish that rod-fishermen do. Seven times! Ye gods! It's as crude as during the war. Whenever we had a leaky depth charge, we used to fire it off and pick up hundreds of fish afterwards in the ship's whaler! What with all this net-fishing and UDS, there won't be a blessed salmon in the river in a couple of years' time!'

Darkly silent, the brothers bury their faces in their pints. They are not quite certain whether this is mere banter, for they have only been in the village a year or two. Their seine-netting is their livelihood, or at least part of it, although with salmon costing £4 a pound — smoked salmon more like £7 a pound — in the shops, they don't do badly. They feel that the 'old codgers' are simply indulging in a rich man's pastime ('Rich! On my pension!' the Brigadier would say) with their annual jaunts to Scotland and their dainty messing about with flies. They could never appreciate that fly-fishing was a far more skilled business in its way than the relatively crude method of simply dragging fish put in an all-embracing net.

And as for the old codgers — old buffers sometimes, and old unmentionables when the goading has gone too far — the Brigadier and the Captain are undoubtedly professional in their outlook, even if their fishing is for sport. What is more, it can be immensely hard work. Yet both of them, each in his seventies, goes about it with a verve that would have been approved of by William Scrope, whom the Brigadier is always fond of quoting (much more than Izaak Walton).

'Dangling a line with a bent pin in the water!' scoffs Frank. 'Kid's play!'

It is now the Brigadier's turn to rise and he doesn't even pause to wipe the Guinness from his moustache.

'Kid's play, Frank! You've obviously never handled a salmon-rod! You've got to have arms like a boxer's to handle an eighteen-foot rod, maybe for an hour on end, with a master-great salmon at the end of the line, pulling like a wild horse with the lasso round its neck!'

Whether he realized it or not, the excited old warrior was quoting almost word for word his beloved Scrope, while Captain RN nodded vigorously in support.

'You've got to keep your arms up high, so that your line clears the rocks! One moment you're rushing into the river, next backing out sharp, and all the time keeping your line and reel right! By Gad, kid's play indeed! Anyway, you two, have another pint before you go off to your fell work . . . '

The Brigadier and the Captain are also professional in the way that they dress their own flies, with dexterous fingers a seamstress would envy. I am full of admiration, when occasionally I come across these old cronies and rivals busy about their tray of feathers as they sit in the Brigadier's gun-room, as he still calls it. Beautiful feathers and all manner of little bits and pieces, treasured as if they were jewels, are transformed into flies calculated to deceive the most cunning fish. The tail-feathers of cock pheasants for the making of whisks for dry flies; the feathers of mallard, curlew and golden plover, and the hackles of some old barnyard cock whose days of strutting and crowing have ended. There was wool from the backs of Slocum's sheep, and even the flaxy underfur of a jack-hare kept separate in an old envelope for the dubbings of the flies.

'With all the fishing that goes on all over the country, you could set up a regular cottage industry out of all this,' I remark innocently, watching this exquisite work in fascination.

'My dear fellow!' the Brigadier says in shocked tones, unscrewing his eyeglass for a moment to regard me in distaste. 'To make money, do you mean?'

Captain RN merely snorts. If the Murren brothers could have seen and heard all this, I wonder what their comments would have been. But I am quite sure that, albeit grudgingly, they would have admired the handiwork of 'they old codgers'.

JUNE

Every now and then at this time of year (it really ought to be done every year), the Parish Council, prodded by one of its more earnest — some would say troublesome — members, makes a perambulation of our footpaths. Farmers understandably but sometimes unreasonably detest them, and certainly near towns footpaths can be a nuisance, to say the least, with the likelihood of gates being left open or dogs not under control doing far more damage to sheep and lambs than foxes ever do.

Besides, farmers cannot always make the fullest use of fields across which footpaths run; for example, it isn't easy to leave a passage through ploughland that may grow wheat or barley, and you cannot keep a bull — or you should not — in a field on which runs a right of way. Pigs are no exception: I remember some years ago, in another parish, an old lady walking her small dog on a leash across a field in which two or three sows were rooting. They immediately attacked — not her, but the dog — and the old lady, not having the presence of mind to let her pet go, fell to the ground in the *mêlée* and was killed by the pigs.

So, unless someone is concerned enough to keep an eye on things, farmers do not go out of their way to keep a stile in good repair or some boggy patch made passable — and it is surprising how a piece of barbed wire will creep like some growing vine across a gap in a hedge through which a path goes. What is more, farmers are always pretty quick on the draw in claiming that a right of way has not been used regularly.

Some counties are much better than others in keeping up their footpaths and signposting them — especially since the national registration of rights of way, and where the Footpaths Society and the Ramblers' Association are active — but it greatly depends on how much the paths are used. Many of them have simply faded out because people don't walk — except for a minority of enthusiasts. To illustrate that, it is only necessary to look at the National Parks Survey carried out a few years ago, which showed that the majority of visitors never ventured more than a couple of hundred yards from their cars, while a sizeable number just *sat* in theirs and stared at the view (in the intervals of scanning their Sunday newspapers).

In our parish there are not all that many visitors, although one or two farms take in holiday-makers and there are a few B & Bs nearer the main road. So the footpaths are, or were, used mainly by the villagers themselves. One, for instance, runs for a couple of miles across part of three farms and leads to the church and The Lamb. There is the Drover's Road and various others, one of which runs through the syndicate's property, to their fury — about which Reg Dredge had words with Keeper Comstock, if you remember. I have a feeling that the Parish Council chairman is going to dodge that one till the last — perhaps in the hope that the weather will break and we shall not be able to investigate it.

Our perambulation of the footpaths is mostly a pleasant, leisurely affair, spread over two or three evenings — snatched from gardening and farming activities. Having time for a friendly stroll is very different from an ordinary Parish Council meeting, which largely consists of taking note of a circular from the NFU or the Forestry Commission, and realizing in general that there is nothing to do and nothing that can be done. But now in the evening calm, you discuss the crops, admire somebody's cattle, talk about the Test Match, and you get a different view, literally and metaphorically, of the parish: the way Hatchetty Ridge thrusts out like a gigantic ship sailing into the green sea of Westermain Woods, which in turn curl like an enormous wave ready to crash down on Foggy Bottom, the way the gilded cockerel stands out so proudly on the church tower when you are looking up at it from among Slocum's young swedes, in which partridges are creaking anxiously. And the fields themselves: one or two of the village members know their names — Walnut-tree, Long Acre, Burnt Tree,

. . . the path that looks
As if it led on to some legendary
Or fancied place where men have wished to go
And stay; till, sudden, it ends where the wood ends

EDWARD THOMAS

Huggins, Betsy's Down, Plague Ground (this latter from a tradition that a mass grave exists there from the fearful pest of a past age), and so on — a handful of mementoes from a more personal, intimate time.

But just as the placid English countryside has begun to have its soothing effect on us, with the bell-ringers practising and the swifts screaming above us, as if to draw attention to the sound, just as we are beginning to relish the prospect of a matey pint in The Lamb, our parochial duty done, an 'explosion' occurs.

A padlock! One of the gates on the footpath leading from Nut-tree Corner to Puddles has been chained and locked!

Buzzing comments from some members.

A cry of outrage from the earnest member.

A defensive mutter from the agricultural member, a friend and natural ally of the farmer whose property has been so peremptorily barred.

'It's a bloody outrage! He hasn't got the slightest right to block this footpath! We'll have to do something about it, Mr Chairman!'

'You can't blame the man! He's had vasty trouble with folk leaving thiccy gate open! Last straw was when Hussey's heifers got in. They went gallivanting round so that Bert's poor old bull was fair mazed! Couldn't do his stuff for months afterwards, and Hussey got about two hundred quids' worth of service free!'

'Farmers! They're all the same! All take and no give! Anyway, that padlock is coming off if I have to use a hacksaw on it myself! You've stolen the entire country! Look at the damage you've done! Thousands of miles of hedgerows bulldozed! Thousands of acres of woodland destroyed! Killed off our bees with your filthy chemicals! And you get paid for it all — by me! By the likes of me!'

'All to keep you in cheap food, that's what, maister . . . '

Growl — snarl — grinding of teeth. It is a fallacy to imagine that farmers are universally liked in the countryside. The countryman has, appropriately enough, a more down-to-earth attitude than perhaps the townsman has.

In the surrounding meadows the cows interrupt their munching to gaze wide-eyed. Magpies rattle a warning that deranged human-beings are abroad. A blackbird plunges shrieking away like some maiden lady drawing up her skirts. It takes the chairman all his tact to calm things down. Sullenly we leave the matter for the time-being ('But I shall certainly raise it at the next Parish Council meeting!'). That once pleasantly anticipated pint has turned really bitter in prospect.

Worse is to come.

In due course we turn into the Drover's Lea. Stonechats clack fussily among the gorse-bushes, which are still spangled with gold. Moorhens utter their metallic calls from the willows overhanging the pond. A heron takes off with stately indifference. Rabbits show their white scuts. In the distance, the alternative life-style young couple go out to fetch their chocolate-coloured, flop-eared Nubian goats. They may even find some chanterelles on the way — there's a certain place where they grow quite well — and I fear they have been discovered.

'Sixteen acres of good land gone to waste!' declares the agricultural member, legs straddled, hands in breeches pockets, blade of grass in mouth. 'If I had my way, I'd fence 'un in, plough 'un up, and I'd get forty ton of dredge corn off of 'un first season! Can't think how 'twas never enclosed long back!'

This time the eruption makes our chairman turn quite pale. It almost seemed as if the earnest member was about to commit physical assault and battery — and now he is joined by the other members, who are equally indignant. Everyone knows, of course, that there is not the faintest chance, or danger, of that piece of common land being fenced in, but the mere idea touches a raw, atavistic nerve among the villagers. We are all well aware that little material use is made of the Drover's Lea — people walk their dogs on it, ride on it, skate on the pond in the rarely suitable winter, gather mushrooms on it, a few animals are grazed on it, and folk such as old Annie Medlicott, looking as if she had emerged straight out of Corot's *A la recherche des fagots*, gathers firing sticks in her apron. But the simple rhetorical suggestion of fencing it in smacks too much of the piratical past when so many villagers were deprived of their commons by various enclosure acts that made the fat fatter.

We think of the motorcar as the arch-villain in changing country-life (and it is ironical to read Arthur Young who, writing more than two hundred years ago, blamed better roads and faster coach-travel for much of the depopulation of the countryside, 'when a country fellow, one hundred miles from London, jumps on a coach box in the morning, and for eight or ten shillings gets to town by nightfall'); but probably few people nowadays realize what a radical effect those enclosures had. They may have led to more 'efficient' farming, but they utterly changed the way of life of English villagers. Literature is studded with references to this. The matter was well pointed up by John Byng in his diaries, when he enquired of a country labourer whether the local common had been long enclosed.

'Ah, lackaday, sir, that was a sad job; and ruined all us poor volk. And those who then gave it, now repent it.'

'Why so?' asked Byng.

'Because we had our garden, our bees, our share of a flock of sheep, the feeding of our geese; and could cut turf for our fuel. Now all that is gone!'

And to quote Arthur Young again: 'By nineteen out of twenty Enclosure Acts the poor are injured, in some cases grossly injured. The poor in these parishes may say, and with truth, "Parliament may be tender of [concerned for] property; all I know is, *I had a cow, and an Act of Parliament has taken it from me*".'

Mind you, there were of course plenty who favoured enclosure of common land in the interests of 'progress', that shibboleth of doubtful value and hypocrisy unconfined. One Augustan agricultural pundit denounced the commons as 'seminaries of a lazy, thieving sort of people. Their sheep are poor, tattered and poisoned with rot, their cattle starved, tod-bellied runts, neither fit for the dairy nor the yoke.'

And as far back as Elizabethan times, when enclosure began, Thomas Tusser declared:

> The Champion* robbeth by night,
> And prowleth and filcheth by day:
> Himself and his beasts out of sight,
> Both spoileth and taketh away
> Not only thy grass but thy corn
> Both after and e'er it be shorn.

That was typical, for the advocates of enclosure set out to denigrate the countryman who depended on his share of common land to maintain his independence. And there is no question but that the enclosures through the centuries did largely destroy the independence of the cottager, turning him into a wage-earner and job-seeker. (Our generation is not by a long chalk the only one

---

*unfenced, common land

Although we tend to think of sheep as man's first attempt to domesticate or exploit animals, his association with bees is probably far older. Long before he started to keep bees in hives, he robbed wild bees of their honey. In Spain there are cave paintings near Valencia showing primitive tribesmen doing just that. In Egypt, bees were depicted on tombs and monuments as early as 3500BC. And for long afterwards, in Roman and Saxon times, honey was the chief sugar supply.

with rampant unemployment — it existed on a mass scale after the Napoleonic Wars, for example.) Nobody summed up the question better than George Bourne, so we will let him work for us:

> To the enclosure of the common more than to any other cause may be traced all the changes that have subsequently passed over the village. It was like knocking the keystone out of an arch. The keystone is not the arch; but, once it is gone, all sorts of forces, previously resisted, begin to operate towards ruin, and gradually the whole structure crumbles down. By the peasant system, people derived the necessaries of life from the materials and soil of their own countryside. Now, so long as they had the common, the villagers were in a large degree able to

> conform to this system, the common being, as it were, a supplement to the cottage garden, and furnishing means of extending the scope of the little home industries. It encouraged the poorest labourer to practise, for instance, all those time-honoured crafts which Cobbett, in his little book on Cottage Economy, had advocated as the one hope for labourers. The cow-keeping, the bread-making, the fattening of pigs and curing of hams were carried on here until near the turn of the century as well as turf-cutting on the heath and wheat-growing in the garden. But it was the common that made all this possible. It was only by the spacious 'turn-out' which it afforded that the people were enabled to keep cows and get milk and butter; it was only with the turf-firing cut on the common that they could smoke their hams, hanging them in the wide chimneys over those old open hearths where none but such fuel could be used; and again it was only because they could get furze from the common to heat their bread ovens that it was worth their while to grow a little wheat at home, and have it ground into flour for making bread. With the common, however, they could and did achieve all this . . .

And they could cut pig-litter from the bracken on the common and stack it, and on good woodland common they could fatten their pigs on the pannage of beechmast and acorns and — it was the earnest member carrying on where Bourne had left off. 'D'you know, that in the first thirty years of Queen Victoria's reign nearly fifty per cent of some counties were enclosed?'

The chairman slopes away as we reach the village. In the bar, the agricultural member rolls his eyes and buttonholes the cattle-dealer, taking loud refuge in market prices. Fred Marks takes the chalk at the darts-board, although not many are playing tonight — most villagers are busy in their gardens. A few visiting drinkers misread the atmosphere and think it is all due to them. Black-eyed Susie is too occupied in serving the customers to listen, but she smiles sweetly as the earnest member bemoans the passing of the genuine villager.

'Wouldn't it be marvellous — ' he dreams into his mug, but then his voice takes on a moody tone. 'Ah, well, I suppose the plain fact of the matter is that there are too many of us.'

'Look yur, midear,' said Jim Fallow, impatiently, stooping to grab a handful of dark, splendidly friable soil from his potato patch, the result of maybe generations of careful tending — rich feeding (from how many generations of cow and pig, and probably horse!) — back-breaking work, digging, raking, hoeing, weeding. 'You zee thiccy dirt? That's what du count! That's a fax — 'tis the only blessed thing that matters — together with whatsoever du fall from the sky to goo with 'un, be it zunshine or be it rain!'

He gazed almost reverently at the soil before letting it trickle back through his gnarled fingers, clearly enjoying the feel of the warm, moist 'dirt'. Pay-dirt, indeed!

'Ah, 'tis a kind of magic, that, midear, woulden'ee say now?' said the old man, glancing quizzically at me, to make certain that I wasn't smiling sceptically, which I assuredly was not. 'You put in a leetle tiny seed in that there dirt and 'er swells and grows and keeps us fed!'

We had been arguing about all manner of things, from nuclear war to world population, from Moscow to Karamoja — a conversation into which we had drifted when I went across to Town Cottage to fetch a broody hen Jim's missus was lending me to sit a clutch of duck eggs, which in turn we had been given by Mrs Endacott. But now Jim had clinched it all, and he underlined matters by turning back to his mattock and saying dismissively but cheerfully, 'Well, midear, there's work to be done and old Josey [he meant the owl] will soon be doing his rounds' — and he resumed grubbing out the beautifully clean, white early potatoes, first of the season, which he had been digging. 'Ah, thanks be for my little patch of the old globe, I du say. Reckon it's the most preciousest treasure I du possess. 'Cept for my missus!' he added, with a wink, straightening up again momentarily and glancing at the receding figure of his wife who was shutting up the hen-house.

Maybe they would not all have put it quite as eloquently as Jim, but his was the unspoken attitude of other village gardeners — in fact, of us all. At least we have our gardens! If few of the villagers — the men at least — go to church regularly, they do, in a manner of speaking not as exaggerated as it might seem, worship in their gardens, even if it would never occur to them to put it like that. Indeed, if you did attempt to, they would sidle away from you in the bar of The Lamb rather uneasily and change the subject! But no acolyte was ever more devoted than the villager tending his vegetable plot.

Around many of our cottages there spill age-old rambler roses with their flouncy clusters ('Oh, no man knows through what wild centuries roves back the rose'); pinks, with their old-fashioned fragrance, fill the borders; sweet peas that would have gratified Brother Cupani, who sent them from Sicily 250 years ago, flaunt their prodigal loveliness alongside the artichokes; dahlias, later on, reach up their waxy splendour in time for the Flower Show; and, in the autumn sunshine, michaelmas daisies will join with red admirals and peacocks to paint the air with their colours. But, above all, it is vegetables that stir the cottager. Flowers are all right, but it's vegetables that matter — they are food, life itself, a memory of the independence the countryman once enjoyed. Besides, as Jim would say, 'Bain't they beautiful?' He sometimes teases his wife when she fills the cottage with bunches of sweet williams, marigolds, London pride, or whatever: 'They'm pretty as a picture sure enough, but you cassn't eat them — you cassn't make a sauce of them like you can with mint! Now peas in a pod, they'm like great fat gems, woulden they look well as a necklace, eh? — a bunch of carrots, now, look at that colour, my dear soul — a girt striped marrow, fatter and handsomer than any alderman! And you can eat 'em all, as well as admiring they! Now, they hollyhocks under the window there — tall as a cathedral spire, but they bain't no use to anyone except the bees that do sing their matins in 'em!'

And although he is teasing Mrs Jim, he really does consider his vegetables like that — and, after all, beauty is in the eye of the beholder. The material and the beautiful — what an excellent combination!

Even the compost heaps are a matter of satisfaction. Every single thing, barring bottles and tins and plastic, goes on to them. Tea-leaves, coffee-grounds, banana skins, orange peel, potato peelings. Not a single item is wasted. The only time that Jim frowns is at the thought that in the past most of it would have gone into the pig-bucket. But apart from the satisfaction derived from a vegetable garden, the pride in those neatly banked-up potatoes, the broad beans whose sweet-scented flowers the bumble-bees love, the onions which in autumn, plump and golden, will hang in neatly plaited bunches in the kitchen — apart from all this there is the added spice of rivalry.

Old Jim has had a picking of broad beans already, they say in the pub. 'Corbugger, I've scarcely tilled mine. Or cabbages — like ruddy cannonballs, his Savoys. Reckon they'd stun a chap if you heaved one at him!' The rivalry extends even to matters such as pea-sticks and bean-sticks. These are not always easy to obtain, for not every hedge is either available or suitable, especially with some of the mutilation that has nowadays largely supplanted the hedger's ancient English skill which helped to create much of the charm of the English countryside. If you

My vegetable love should grow
Vaster than empire, and more slow

When he wrote that in the seventeenth century, Andrew Marvell may not have been thinking along modern lines. But, undoubtedly, for many people a vegetable garden is more satisfying than any empire.

know where there is a good supply of sticks, you keep it secret. At certain times, especially towards spring-time, before the leaves put out again, you can sometimes see a car or a van, even a tractor, parked down some by-way leading into one of the Squire's copses, or in the case of some daring folk, alongside the syndicate's woodland, after they have made certain of Keeper Comstock's whereabouts. And presently the same vehicle passes you on its way home, a nice bundle or two of pea-sticks in the open boot or the link-box piled with bean-poles.

But, like democracy, a village garden is a matter of eternal vigilance. There is no lack of other candidates for nature's bounty and man need not imagine that because he tilled the soil and planted the seed, the end-product is exclusively his! (Because they are more enclosed, more 'sanitized' by barren streets and concrete walls, town-gardens are less vulnerable to all the so-called pests that make us realize we cannot take things for granted. As John Ray said in the seventeenth century, it is absurd to think that the universe was made solely for man; the stars do not twinkle just at us!) There are the sleek wood-mice, innocently large-eyed, which will ravage a new-sown row of peas almost before you turn your back; the black fly — the 'Black Army' as we call it — which you can guard against by nipping out the tops of the broad beans to toughen the stems; the carrot fly whose tastes are more catholic than its name suggests, celery and parsnip also being included in its menu; thrips, those brownish-yellow insects that mar your apples and pears; greenfly (do you remember that marvellous year when ladybirds were so prolific?); white fly; red spider mite; cabbage whites, whose caterpillars will make skeletons of your brassicas; eel-worm that will ruin your potatoes if the blight does not.

Above all, there is the never-ending battle against slugs and snails. Jim never wastes money on slug-pellets. He makes slug-traps of old cups or tins sunk level with the soil and filled with beer-dregs or even milk, which collect a gruesome mass of drowned slugs. But even the slugs are not wasted, for they go on to the compost heap — and eventually back into the soil whose fruits they have plundered! But listen, there's my right-hand man at work, says Jim, raising a hand. From the far side of the garden comes a small but persistent tapping, and presently, its beak well laden, a song-thrush flies off, no doubt to feed its second brood of the year. And at the edge of the path is its anvil, a stone around which are strewn dozens of fragments of snail-shells that it has hammered open.

I have my natural allies, too, in the form of slow-worms which gratefully accept the shelter of a piece of corrugated iron in a waste corner, in return for the toll they take of slugs, and hedgehogs which come to the kitchen door most evenings to partake of the bread and milk we put out for them. The trouble is that hedgehogs have tastes other than slugs and snails — including those same slow-worms and also the frogs and toads who do sterling service in helping to control all those myriad creatures we in our subjective attitude call pests!

I am sure, however, that Jim Fallow would agree with Cobbett that the greatest enemies in the garden are the straight back and the gossip . . .

JULY

In spite of all the impersonalization that has taken over in agriculture — the battery hens, the broiler houses, the milking machines, the intensive rearing of calves, and so on — you cannot live in an ordinary country village without being frequently in contact with animals, or at least aware of their presence. Most days, depending on where they are grazing, somebody's cows pass up and down the village street and sometimes manage to snatch a bit of grazing on the green. Recently, during shearing-time, we were more than usually aware of Mr Slocum's flocks, penned up in loud lamentation in his yard, while the shearing-gang went swiftly about their work. Afterwards, the air was heavy with the smell of disinfectant as the sheep underwent one of their twice-yearly dippings against the scab.

Occasionally, however, animal encounters in the village are of a more dramatic kind. One morning an unnerving but fortunately unusual sound could be heard approaching the village from the main road and heading towards Parkside. It was an ambulance, closely followed by PC Keane in his Panda (it's remarkable how often he contrives to be sent our way whenever duty calls — the answer can be found, of course, in The Lamb). Anyway, the cause of this particular visitation was an encounter between Jack Hoggett and Farmer Hussey's Ayrshire bull.

Luckily the bull had been dehorned, and although the village experienced a heart-stopping moment when the ambulancemen carried Jack out on a stretcher, they were reassured by a thumbs-up sign from him, for he had got off comparatively lightly with some nasty bruises and patches of what might be called gravel-rash. Mr Hussey had valiantly gone to the rescue with the almost traditional dung-fork and the two men had managed to scramble to safety.

The incident took place in a corner of the yard, a relatively confined space, which is where most mishaps with bulls occur. A sensible rule, of course, is that you can never be sure of a bull, but generally speaking it is much less aggressive or irritable when out in the field in company with the cows. In any case, the typical massive half-ton bull cannot *run* all that fast, although younger bulls, two or three years old, are always liable to be more troublesome.

But the conventional image of people fleeing for their lives across a field and doing a record high-jump over hedge or gate is more likely to occur in fiction — as, for example, when Johnny Eames went to the rescue of Earl de Guest in Trollope's *The Small House at Allington* and held off the Guestwick champion while his lordship vaulted to safety. And although the Earl was not correct in claiming that his bull was 'a large, horned, innocent lamb of the flock', there was something in his claim that 'he'll never hurt anyone that has not hurt him', even though that particular bull rather contradicted him. Nor had Jack Hoggett ever hurt Hussey's bull, but some years ago there was a somewhat unsavoury old character who lived at Nut-tree Corner on the outskirts of the village who had. He was unkindly known as Fly-blow because of his ill-kempt appearance, or alternatively The Colonel because of his bushy moustache.

At one time Fly-blow used to work for another of the local farmers, but even after he was pensioned off and only did the odd-job or two, the bull in question could tell at two or three hundred yards when he was approaching, for it never forgot the occasional hurt the old man had done to it. It would set to bellowing its vengeful thoughts and trampling around the gateway, so that people would look up and remark that The Colonel must be on parade.

Fly-blow always maintained his innocence and claimed that the original hostility between him and that 'cappernishious old brute', as he called the bull, was when it once attacked him completely without provocation. ''Er eyed me real ugsomely and began to come after I a mite too hurryful. I were in a fair old fantigue, 'cos I were humping a bucket of milk to the calves. So I did dowse 'er in

ABOVE AND OVERLEAF
For many centuries the pig has been one of the most valuable animals for the peasant-farmer. It can forage for a living on ground useless to other stock, grub for roots, live on acorn and beechmast, feed on carrion and household scraps. It can be kept in a confined space, and a sow can have two litters a year of anything up to a dozen piglings a time, even though some of these are so scrinnicky as to earn old folk-names such as nizzledraft, little Josey, pedman or trooeltrype or the better known runt.

the eyes with the milk and then caught 'un a crack on the snout with the bucket!'

It isn't only elephants that have long memories.

Well, fortunately, Jack Hoggett was back the same evening, a bit stiff, and off work for a day or so. The thoughtful PC Keane came out to inquire after his welfare and, considerately reluctant to disturb Mrs Hoggett, he went along to The Lamb to see if Susie could let him know how Jack was progressing.

Although not all animal matters are as dramatic as Jack's mishap, animals can be the cause of bad blood among the villagers — or to put it more fairly and accurately, it is the animals' owners who are the cause, for it is nearly always brought about by broken fences. Incidents of this kind are particularly liable to happen at this time of year when cottage gardening is at its height and we are already beginning to think about the still-distant Flower Show, for flowers and vegetables need much tending of a long-term extent.

Sheep are notoriously restless after their shearing, partly because, if the weather subsequently turns cold or wet, they feel this in their naked state just as much as they suffered from the discomfort of the sun when they were still burdened with their heavy fleeces. Equally, ewes and lambs often become separated at shearing, for their recognition-scent is lessened or distorted. So there is always a number of errant sheep liable to be wandering the village and by-ways — and getting into those precious gardens than which no holy place could be more sacrosanct!

It is also alleged that Cushy Doe, the sexton, connives at all this, for it is said that he is not above letting a few lost sheep graze overnight in the churchyard to save him scything some of the more inaccessible corners, where some particular succulent pasture exists. Personally, I believe this to be a slander, for Cushy is also accused of growing his prize marrows in the vicinity of some of the unmarked graves on the far side of the church. Be that as it may, sheep do get into the graveyard, whence, if so minded, they can hop over the low wall which separates it from the gardens of Church Cottages.

Mrs Endacott: I looked out and I saw they sheep in his garden next door, picking and choosing among his cabbages like some old body looking over a market stall. And I said to myself, you never done me a good turn, not even when Joe was ill . . .' (The garden in question belonged to Mr Counter, the ex-bank manager.)

'But then, as I watched, I did say to mysen, Lizzy Endacott, that bain't being a true Christian. So I sent young Maisie round to warn 'un about they blessed ship.'

Pigs, adorable characters though they are, can, if they trespass, cause fearful depredations akin to some mediaeval scorched earth campaign.

'The guzzling zow of yourn has been rampaging among my 'taters!' Bill Coombe of Owlsfoot raged at Mr Slocum on one famous occasion. 'Next time I'll give her a veast of lead to be chewing on!'

'Don't you dare lay a finger on my Rosebud!' a voice of outrage shrilled from a bedroom window of Town Farm, for Mrs Slocum was in earshot of it all. 'She'm being shown at Fleckham Show next week, and if any harm comes to her, I'll know who's responsible, William Coombe, you!'

'You mark my words, missus,' Bill Coombe had said darkly, slapping his wellingtons with a hazel switch, 'happen there won't be no more prize winning for that yur zow of yourn if the brute comes snouting my way agen!' At which there was the most almighty crash, which nearly shattered the panes, as Mrs Slocum slammed down the window in a mixture of distress and indignation.

But undoubtedly the most celebrated happening in the village concerning animals was the affair of Maudie Coombe's geese (Maudie was a cousin of Bill Coombe, for there are endless ramifications and permutations among the village families). She used at times to turn the geese out on the village green, a gander and nearly a dozen geese — for why let the grazing go to waste? Now, at times, nothing can be more aggressive than geese, and Maudie's were a supreme example of this. Anyone passing by on foot was liable to be attacked. Led by the gander the flock would go charging at their target — they could never get properly airborne, but would labour in a pandemonium of wings a few feet above the ground.

Many people became reluctant to run this feathered gauntlet. They complained to the Parish Council to no avail, whereupon somebody, still unidentified though suspected, took the matter in hand by means of some cunningly poisoned bread, for geese are notoriously greedy. The hostile wings were stilled, the gaggling voices no longer struck terror among the old and the young. When Maudie went out one evening to drive in her handsome if unpopular flock, she found them, every single bird, stretched out in what Sam Dredge called 'rigorous morbid'.

In bygone times (in the ancient days of the village constable), stray animals would have ended up in the village pound, where they would stay until redeemed by their owner. Now overgrown with nettles and docks, brambles and ash saplings, this circular enclosure, walled by a five-foot bank of earth and stones, still exists. But the Parish Council has recently had the bright idea of clearing it and putting a bench or two in it, so that old folk and others so inclined can go and sit there of a clement afternoon.

'What be the use of that?' demands Sam Dredge, First World War veteran. 'Us coulden zee over the top. We'd be like gunners squatting in a sandbag emplacement. 'Zides, 'tis tu far from The Lamb, I rackon!'

The village lanes are at their best now. Apart perhaps from slight nuisances to impatient motorists in the shape of pot-holes or bosky corners you can't see around, we benefit from the general adversity, for less and less attention is paid to the by-ways where we live. Once upon a time we had a parish roadman, Joe Beaworthy. He would, with scythe and sickle and twirg (a short forked stick with one branch cut off close, invaluable in grasping the foliage as he cut it with the sickle), work his way steadily through the parish and when he reached the far end of it under Starvation Hill it was time to start all over again, especially at Joe's pace — and nobody begrudged him his frequent stops at The Lamb.

When he retired, the RDC (as it then was) took over and occasionally a gang of council workmen — five of them to make certain the sixth was getting on with it — would arrive to 'do' the banks. For a short time chemical sprays were used to keep down the 'weeds' until valiant opposition, spearheaded by the Women's Institute, brought a halt to that. Nowadays, apart from the hedge-cutting farmers are obliged to carry out, we have thankfully been left alone to a great extent and long may it remain. Praise God for wilderness, as Gerard Manley Hopkins said. Discounting the occasional useless token dab of tar and chippings, the County Council is only interested in the main roads, and I, for one, do not mind in the least. Besides, those pot-holes are as good as any ramp in slowing down cars.

The upshot of all this is that some of the lanes at certain times, especially just now, as high summer surges nearer in its great scented leafy waves, are a galaxy of wild flowers, bold pennons defying (successfully we hope) any official vandal to come and slash down their passing loveliness. Lady's smock lingers on while the golden-starred agrimony takes over from it. The delicate pale-yellow starry clusters of lady's bedstraw mingle with the tiny snapdragons of toadflax (touch-me-not, its other picturesque name). Willow-herb begins to appear in dense stands against a background of unfurling bracken. Treacle mustard thrusts up through an old pile of road-sand and is flanked by fumitory, once so dear to the ancient physicians. Honeysuckle, dog-roses, trailing roses, all add their marvellous offerings, neighboured by meadow sweet, apt name for this flower so redolent of English summer. Foxgloves stand in magnificent ranks, their handsomeness as fine as their name is evocative. And in Mr Slocum's nearby oats, languidly dreamy-looking poppies gently nod their heads, as if in conversation with the thistles that guard them!

The creamy bunches of the elder top the hedges. Wayfaring-tree and guelder-rose, danewort and mullein flank the gateways. Red campion is not yet over, white campion lasts longer, and presently village children will amuse themselves by popping the calyxes of bladder-campion by smacking them smartly on the back of their hands. Wild carrot and wild parsley raise their umbrellas; bugle, yellow archangel, purple dead nettle, and dozens of other floral stars light the way along this botanical paradise. And if you follow this particular lane as far as Huggins — a bit farther, actually — you will find a patch of ground thick with wild garlic, while the adjoining bramble brakes are festooned with the sinister but handsome flowers of the deadly nightshade which later on will put forth its glossy black berries, big as cherries — in fact, they used to be called naughty man's cherries, for they are direly poisonous. That particular spot is the Plague Ground, which we mentioned earlier, and it is always reckoned that belladonna — that other, more stately alias of the deadly nightshade — flourishes where once human habitations stood. But they say that about the ubiquitous nettle, too.

And first thing this morning, while greenfinch and white-throat and redstart flit and scold and chack anxiously, these flowery lanes are brightened not only with the riotous colours of all the varied petals, but by the voices of some of the village children from the primary school. Today is their end of term exhibition and one or two of the classes are for wild flowers of different species and colours and sizes. And in gathering wild flowers you have to leave them until the very last moment, for it wasn't only Flecker's Yasmin who realized that 'gathered flowers are dead'.

Half a century ago, Walter de la Mare could write rather sadly:

> Nowadays, our minds and their contents, like our clothes, seem to tend to be more and more alike; and most children are taught in school — what most children are taught in school. A lively and happy country girl, when I asked her the name of a star-clustering wild flower flourishing everywhere on her farmland, replied that she didn't know, and explained with a smile 'At school, you know, I never cared for Nature study'. The very phrase was like a knell. It was as if a child after politely listening to 'how many miles to Babylon?' or 'Ride-a-cock-horse' or 'The Queen was in her parlour', had muttered, 'I'm sorry, you know! but I can't abide that William Wordsworth'.

He would find a difference today, for although the circle has not turned fully it has turned quite a long way, thanks to a general if belated interest in and concern for nature. There are more books on the subject (now of course being barbarously cut down in schools) and intimate television programmes — but, needless to say, both depend on interested teachers. In our village school Miss Rix is certainly that — the children say she's 'special' — and the class-room is decorated with charts of flowers and birds and 'toadstools' augmented by the children's own interpretations. There might be truth in Romeo's words:

> What's in a name? that which we call a rose
> By any other name would smell as sweet;

In this instance the race is not so much to the swift as the nimble and sure-footed. To stand on your own feet was never so much needed as here.

Mankind 'danced' long before music was evolved, for we can dance to the tune of the singing of the blood we hear coursing through our veins.

Is the gentleman contemplating the future that has been forecast for him or merely wondering whether to cross the fortune-teller's palm with a cupro-nickel piece?

nevertheless, it surely heightens the interest to know what a flower is called, and also the functions of stamen, calyx, sepal, and pistil, and in addition what vital work the bee does at the same time as 'he doth suck his sweet'.

What has largely disappeared or been forgotten are the old country nicknames for wild flowers: dead man's bells for the foxglove (a nice allusion, one supposes, to the fact that the plant contains the poison digitalis); butter and eggs for toadflax (although I prefer 'touch-me-not'); cuckoo bread for wood sorrel; love-man for the goose-grass that clings on to you so affectionately, and so on.

'And Flower of Constantinople for campion. Lungwort is Mary's tears, did you know? They say the spots on its leaves were caused by the tears she shed at the crucifixion. And the purple orchis is called Gethsemane, because it was growing at the foot of the cross and drops of Christ's blood fell on its leaves and they have kept those marks ever since.'

All this comes from Miss Rix, for *she* has never forgotten those names, being somewhat of a Fundamentalist, as we might say, in country matters. She had come along now to accompany and help the children, but she was also in search of elder flowers which she was gathering for her wine. She is a proselytizer as well — and I don't mean about religion.

'I know you brew beer,' she says, hooking on her pebble glasses again, which have become disarranged as she reaches up with a stick to bend down the creamy, frothy blossoms (she is immensely tall as well as bulky and has no difficulty in stretching up to the most inaccessible places), 'but you really should try elder-flower. It has such a delicate flavour. *Much* better than elder berry, which I consider rather coarse and syrupy. Such a *gentle* colour, too. If you would care to have my recipe — '

Suddenly a shrill chorus rings out.

'Miss! Miss! There's a big brown bird in the field with a broken wing!'

'It's a partridge, Miss! Come quick! We might catch 'un!'

Like so many large people, Miss Rix is surprisingly light on her feet. Before the excited voices have ceased, she has opened the gate and has joined the children in time to see a hen partridge go fluttering and crippling away along the edge of the oatfield.

'Shall we catch it, Miss?'

'Perhaps we could mend it!'

But while the cunning mother partridge continues to scutter and tumble along, inviting pursuit, and no doubt her late brood are scattering to safety unseen, Miss Rix explains it all to *her* brood. The partridge is not injured, it is just playing its usual trick of pretending to be crippled, in order to distract the children — and it would have been the same in the case of a marauding fox or dog — and to give the buff-coloured, quicksilver, still flightless 'cheepers' time to escape.

In his *Cottage Economy*, published in 1821, William Cobbett declared:

> Understand me clearly here, however; for it is the duty of parents to give, if they be able, book-learning to their children having *first* taken care to make them capable of earning their living by *bodily labour*. When that object has once been secured, the other may, if the ability remain, be attended to. But I am wholly against children wasting time in the idleness of what is called *education*; and particularly in schools over which the parents have no control, and where nothing is taught but the rudiments of servility, pauperism, and slavery.

So much for education as the liberator of mankind! But how extraordinary it is to read that, and then 'sit-in' (as I have done) at one of Miss Rix's lessons, for Miss Rix is not only 'special', as the children put it, she is a 'natural' — a natural teacher, far in advance of any paper qualifications she has. Among the village children (for some years now this applies only to those of primary age, for the others go to Fleckham) there is no 'creeping like snail unwillingly to school', and some of them go to extra lessons given freely after school-hours by Miss Rix, notably in music, and the now fashionable recorder is frequently to be heard piping out its pleasantly mediaeval note.

Sometimes she cajoles people into displaying their particular skill or interest to the children. Once she persuaded Mr Lugg, a retired policeman living in Fleckham, to come and demonstrate the art of dowsing or water-divining for which he is renowned (in the past he was often employed by farmers anxious to find a new water-supply). Usually water-diviners prefer to work completely on their own, but there was Mr Lugg, attended at a discreet distance by the children, quartering one of the Town Farm meadows, a Y-shaped hazel divining-rod gripped firmly in his upturned palms, elbows tucked close to his sides, and waiting to feel that strange tension that would, at the first hint of underground water, turn the rod, twist it almost, in his hands in spite of his grip.

Another time, by arrangement, Miss Rix took the children along to Captain RN to see his collection of old tools and farm implements — an ancient pit-saw, wooden yokes, a seedlip for broadcast sowing, a winnowing-machine which still thunderously responded to the turning handle. But the outstanding success of that live lesson was the demonstration the Captain gave with a flail.

I was present on that particular occasion and was fascinated both by the way the Captain had mastered the skill and the deceptively easy, almost lazy action that was needed, for it was obviously hard work for wrists and arms and shoulders. He lifted the hand-staff slightly above the level of his shoulders, then, bringing over the swingel which was attached by an iron bolt to the slotted top of the hand-staff, let its own weight carry it down flat on to the bundle of straw he had 'borrowed' from Mr Slocum. It was all a matter of timing and rhythm.

If ever a teacher struck sparks from her pupils it is Miss Rix, who, for forty years now, has been a respected figure in the village. In fact, a remarkable fact when you come to think of it, she has been a village school-teacher for getting on for half the time our school has been in existence. It was, in common with hundreds of others all over the country, built a little more than a hundred years ago as a result of the Education Act of 1870, the work of that Gladstonian supporter, W.E. Forster, a Quaker who became an ardent churchman, and of course for long the influence of the church on the village school was paramount — a fact much resented by some people such as the Methodists.

The village school was, at first, resented also for other reasons. The parents would have agreed with old Cobbett, for compulsory education prevented children from earning money, even though this was a pittance, at such jobs as bird-scaring or minding the cows or as plough-boys (Cobbett's own father earned two pence a day at that). But even those small earnings were important in days when living-standards were so wretched that village folk often had to mortgage half their pig to pay the baker or the miller, and women and children went gleaning after the harvest to win a few wisps of wheat or oats to provide a bushel or two of flour.

But after this early prejudice, the school came to represent the beating heart and future of the village, perhaps far more than the church did. That, of course, was in an age when the village was still a living entity and not the artificial creation it largely is today — an age when children gradually took over from their parents, continued the same traditions, continued the same crafts and jobs. Going away to school, even to the neighbouring market-town as they mostly do now, they cannot possibly take the same interest in or have the same concern for the village. Ostensibly their horizons have broadened immeasurably, their ambitions, too. One sometimes wonders, however, whether, if the so-called economic climate continues to worsen for the unforeseeable future, the village, as that same living entity, with local crafts and jobs, will not be revived. It might mean a less affluent time, but possibly a happier and more meaningful one.

Alas and doubly alas, the question will soon no longer obtain in our village, for the incomparable Miss Rix, exemplar of all that education stands for if it means not only book-learning but the enlightenment of the spirit, is soon to retire, and this coincides with strong rumours that our village school is to be closed down and the 'infants', as their seniors already are, bussed to Fleckham. If the motorcar has had a radical effect on traditional village life, so too has the closure of so many country schools — in the interests of a false economy.

And no doubt our school itself will be sold and converted into a dwelling to be occupied by some commuter whose proud address will be The Old Schoolhouse.

AUGUST

Nothing matters this month except *the* match; perhaps we should say THE MATCH. Preparations for the Flower Show, the WI outing to the seaside, late hay, early harvest — all pale into insignificance in comparison. The red baler in Hussey's field looks like some resentful beast foiled in its depredations. The monstrous blue and yellow combine harvester stands silent as the contract-driver watches from his tall perch. By the end of the day the local herds are lowing their heads off, protesting that milking-time is overdue. Although this may not apply to the country in general, to the village, cricket means far more than football does. In our village, football is played with much fervour but there is often difficulty in raising a team, while matches are attended by a meagre handful of supporters. Not only is cricket played, in principle, at a more clement time (notwithstanding Byron's libel — 'The English winter — ending in July, to recommence in August'), but its atmosphere is infinitely more relaxing and it is astonishing how many deck-chairs adorn the boundary at times, and the sleepers in the nearby graveyard are not alone.

More important, cricket embraces a far wider cross-section (an uncomfortable metaphor, admittedly) of the village. 'Everybody' takes part. Mrs Endacott and her cohorts cut sandwiches and brew enormous urns of tea in the miniscule pavilion. Mr Watchet, the Parish Council clerk, keeps the score ('I notches 'em up,' he says, with a nice touch evoking memories of Broadhalfpenny Down). The ex-bank manager umpires, complete with straw boater and white coat ('If he wore a striped apron,' declares Mrs Endacott, unkindly, 'you couldn't tell 'un from the Noshington butcher' — but, then, she has parted company from Mrs ex-bank manager, for whom she no longer 'does').

As for the players, Reg Dredge, as we have proudly stated before, is captain, while the Rector opens the batting with him and also bowls a cunning off-break. Alf Slocum keeps wicket, his long nose almost protruding through the stumps. The garagist is our chief all-rounder. Jeremy Dredge can always be relied upon, as too can Alf Futcher, the Squire's cowman. Mr Bernstein of the Barton turns out in immaculate 'creams', as he will call them, and never gets higher in the batting order than number eight, in spite of his generous subscriptions to the club. The position of last man fluctuates between Mr Scales of the shop and the Rector's nephew, Martin.

And the Squire is president and lets us play in his meadow behind the church.

Although the village meets stronger teams, the highlight of the season, the match that really matters, is the encounter with Great Noshington.

'Pray heaven we have a scorcher so's we can truly frizzle they scallywags,' says Mrs Endacott, as if she were a Rachel Hayhoe striding out at Lord's, and she polishes the tea urns with the zest of a Holding polishing the ball on his thigh.

If not a scorcher, we did at least have a pleasantly balmy day, with the swallows hawking low across the fields amd the swifts screaming around the church tower, as if in excitement at the prospect. But first thing in the morning there was a nasty moment. Jill Dunch came screeching under Alf Futcher's window that 'they blessed heifers of Mr Bernstein be in cricket medder!'

Action stations! Still looping on his braces, Alf rushed across the green and through the churchyard, followed by his wife's strident machine-gun reprobations that she had 'told 'un a'dunnamany times to mend that fence!' It really is quite remarkable how such a tiny woman can produce so many decibels. Fortunately, however, Jill had spotted the errant heifers early on when she was out mushrooming. They had only penetrated the outfield, and hadn't got anywhere near the pitch. Alf not only set to and mended the fence, but he got Mr Bernstein to shift the heifers to another field to be on the safe side.

Long before two o'clock, the first motorcars from outlying parts began to arrive. The village was gratified at the sight of half a dozen of the Squire's weekend guests turning up. The deck-chairs were being carried through the short-cut of the graveyard, their owners looking like so many colourful pall-bearers.

'Where's Alf Slocum?' Reg muttered, as the team gradually mustered.

'He were still baling Long Meadow, when I had my dinner,' said Fred Marks.

For a moment, anxiety about our wicket-keeper was forgotten. Suddenly, in a menacing roar, a convoy of vehicles came bustling up the hill like a motorized division about to take the village by storm!

The visitors — what a euphemism for those momentarily most hated men in the entire realm — had arrived, to the wonder and dark surmise of various small boys, who nudged each other knowingly.

On the steps of The Lamb a gaggle of villagers stood, stonily surveying the rival players more like a posse of vigilantes than a reception committee. With a boldness savouring of recklessness, two or three of the Great Noshington eleven pushed past them to get in a hasty pint before the pub closed.

'Brought the reverend to pray for 'em, I suppose,' observed Fred, nodding at the Noshington curate.

'Your scorer'll need his pocket calculator when we start flogging the leather,' retorted one of the visitors, leering at Black-eyed Susie, who had taken over the bar for the last few minutes when Jeremy rushed off to change.

It was perhaps as well that PC Keane now arrived on the scene, zipping along in his Panda. By turning smartly off through the archway of The Lamb, he just avoided colliding head-on with a demented tractor that came roaring through the village from the other end, scattering Daisy Westaway's ducks, which flung themselves hysterically into the brook.

Our wicket-keeper had arrived, signs of his morning's work in the hayfield still festooning his hair.

As it happened, Great Noshington won the toss and batted first. For a while, however, Mr Watchet was in no need of a pocket calculator. His little bowling-squares consisted of nothing but a series of ⁚ ⁚ ⁚ s, which he transformed into rows of neat Ṁ s, although young Derrick had been kept moderately active hanging up the tin numbers thanks to a couple of wides from Reg, a no-ball from Arthur Trump, the jobbing gardener, and two byes that slipped through the wicket-keeper's hands.

But the sleepers were dragged back from the brink when a thunder of feet and a stertorous gasping warned them that the ball was coming their way. It was the first boundary of the afternoon and a disconcerting moment for the Brigadier as the ball rattled menacingly against his deck-chair. 'Thought it was Inkerman all over again,' he quipped, adjusting his panama and folding his crane-like legs. From then on Great Noshington progressed if not evenly, at least steadily. Twenty — one — twelve, the score-board read. Thirty-five — two — nineteen. Thirty-seven — three — nought. Forty-four — four — seven. The village supporters began to murmur appreciatively. The Squire was seen nodding sagely at his guests. The Rector had got into a winning groove.

Then the Great Noshington captain — the butcher whom Mrs Endacott had compared with the ex-bank manager — took charge. He speedily forced Reg to take the Rector off. Another two overs and Jeremy put on his sweater. Mr Watchet could well have done with a pocket calculator and for a long time the only figures Derrick had to change were the top ones. Uneasily the village glanced at the score-board but gave grudging applause when three black and white tin plates were hanging from their hooks. One of the Squire's guests drew dark looks when he cried vociferously 'Jolly good show!' — being under the impression that the home side was batting.

In G.M. Trevelyan's words, 'the institution of Justices of the Peace, local gentry appointed by the Crown to govern the neighbourhood in the King's name, was a move away from inherited feudal jurisdiction.' And chief among these J.P.s was always the Squire.

It was exactly tea-time when the visitors were finally prised out, in their very last over, with a total of one hundred and eighty-four on the board, the butcher seventy-one not out. The village had a fight on its hands.

The village knows how to fight, however, especially against the arch-foe. 'Us'll frizzle they scallywags,' muttered Mrs Endacott, prowling round the trestle tables dispensing sinister looking tea as if she could cheerfully empty the scalding hot contents of her enamel jug down the necks of the visitors.

To begin with, it really did look as if we would frizzle them. The Rector and Reg hooked, slashed, missed, cut and poked with an aplomb that meant the sleepers in the graveyard were on their own, with no support from the occupants of the deck-chairs. Only a reluctant finger from the ex-bank manager brought the partnership to an end. His place on the Parish Council may well be endangered at the next election as a result. Our progress continued, however, and ninety-one runs were on the board before the third wicket fell.

Then disaster struck, literally and metaphorically. Again the enemy captain took charge. He came on to bowl at the pavilion end and some wag asked him if he had come back for another cup of tea, he took such an inordinately long run. The titters soon turned to gasps of dismay. Almost brushing aside the ex-bank manager, like a Croft dealing with a New Zealand umpire, the Great Noshington butcher charged up to the crease and slammed the ball down so hard you would have expected it to be buried in the pitch. The opposite happened. The ball flew up as if set off by a detonator and, eluding the flailing bat of Alf Futcher, struck him with a sickening crack on the side of the head.

If the ball wasn't buried in the pitch by that vicious short delivery, it is a wonder poor Alf was not, for he went down like a barn door falling from its hinges. A ghastly split-second's silence ensued before the entire Great Noshington eleven and half the spectators gathered around the recumbent figure. An audible sigh of relief went up as Alf got shakily to his feet, supported by the enemy wicket-keeper and their umpire, a sigh punctuated by an irate screech from Alf's missus.

'You bloody murderer!' she yelled, dancing up and down behind the Squire's contingent, who looked around in considerable alarm. 'You and your bumpings! I'd like to use one of your own cleavers on 'ee!'

Mrs Futcher's own attacks on her husband were frequent and notorious; if the wind was in the right direction they could be heard at Nut-tree Corner. But it was a case of no other tiger. Meanwhile, Alf had been led back to the pavilion for the collective ministrations of the village matrons. He brushed aside the soothing wet towels and liniments they tried to apply to him.

'Yur, Susie!' he called out huskily. 'Ask your dad if you can nip back to The Lamb and bring I a jar of scrumpy. That'll set me right!'

'I'll give you a hand,' volunteered PC Keane, properly indifferent in an emergency to the licensing hours of the land, and hastened back with Black-eyed Susie through the graveyard (no doubt hoping for the day when he would accompany her down the aisle).

As so often happens after such an incident, fortunes changed. Unnerved by the accident, we suffered a collapse. Intimidation by the unrepentant butcher of Great Noshington accounted for several wickets; a hopeless misunderstanding between Mr Bernstein and Charley Westaway produced a demoralizing Boycott-style run-out, and a dubious decision by the visitors' umpire all contributed to the village being brought swiftly from cosy anticipation of triumph to the verge of defeat.

Then a dogged stand, attended by some good fortune, which the brave always deserve, began to raise our hopes again. It was as if we dared to lift our heads above the parapet once more. Thatcher Dredge was still there, as defiant as

It seems odd that the cricket pitch remains the same length as it was in Queen Anne's reign. In those days men weren't nearly as athletic: they could not run as fast as they do nowadays and they bowled underhand, trundling the ball along the ground. The Holdings and the Lillees of today have a disproportionate advantage.

any captain on the bridge of his sinking ship. Last man in was the Rector's nephew who, with stubborn good sense, kept out what bowling he received, maybe with the help of an inward prayer from his uncle, and, with some heart-stopping singles, dodged as much as he could, leaving the real grafting to Reg.

It was young Derrick's gleeful joy 'to add to golden numbers, golden numbers', to use the words of Thomas Dekker, who may or may not have been acquainted with cricket. At every run he slapped on a new number plate with a crash of triumphant cymbals! Even Cushy Doe had abandoned his scythe in the churchyard and was peering over the wall like some eternal sleeper roused by the excitement.

One hundred and seventy-eight for eight!

Six runs to win! One over to go!

Sir Henry Newbolt should have been there properly to have savoured the hush that fell, if not over the close, at least over the Squire's meadow. But that hush was cruelly shattered. Up went young Martin's head . . . and down went all three stumps with a veritable death-rattle. The groan that went up was so deep that it must surely have been joined by those sleepers in the graveyard. The sexton had disappeared from view as if he could bear to watch no more.

'Give I a bat! I be going out!' declared Alf, staggering from his chair, beside which there stood a now almost empty enamel jug of scrumpy.

'My dear Alf, you're not fit to!' remonstrated the Rector, wincing at the egg-shaped swelling on Alf's temple.

'Those buggers an't a gooing to cheat us, Reverend!' was Alf's response, and the Rector didn't bat an eyelid.

With a final guggling pull at his 'jar', Alf, nodding in commiseration at the incoming Martin, walked, somewhat like Agag, towards the wicket. As the assembled Great Noshington eleven gazed stonily towards him, he put one in mind of the lonely but indomitable sheriff in *High Noon* walking down Main Street, expecting a hail of bullets at any moment.

Our collective hearts sank as he seemed to stagger a little, and even more when he came to a halt, but that was only to tighten his pads which had been left flapping loosely in his hurry to get to the crease. An earnest consultation with Skipper Reg, and Alf took guard. The Great Noshington plumber was bowling, medium-paced, around the wicket, swinging-in-the-air stuff which had foxed several of our batsmen.

The first ball Alf poked at with the air of a man playing blindman's buff, but fortunately didn't get a touch. The second was pitched almost nearer to point than the batsman, but the Great Noshington umpire unblushingly declined to call a wide. The churchyard mutterings started up again. Even Mrs Futcher was gnawing her fingernails, while the Squire's lady was nervously clasping and unclasping her handbag.

One ball to go. Six runs still to win. We would never do it. Last year's defeat would go unrevenged. Only a six would do it, and only one ball to go, except in the unlikely event of the Great Noshington umpire calling a no-ball. A raven flew over, croaking dismally.

Up trundled the plumber. Out stepped Alf, swinging his bat like a Geoff Capes throwing the hammer. Bat met ball with that satisfying, inimitable *clunk*, a sound in the same evocative category as that of drawing a cork.

'By Jove!' cried the usually undemonstrative Squire, jumping to his feet but sitting down immediately when he realized that he was impeding somebody's view. Followed by half a hundred pairs of eyes, the ball continued on its triumphant parabola. Now it had reached the apex of its course, now it was descending gloriously towards the boundary, by which time at least three Great Noshington fielders were converging in desperate hope.

But far more ancient and dark
The combe looks since they killed the badger there,
That most ancient Briton of English beasts.

EDWARD THOMAS

It has been said that the kitchen must be the first foundation of a house. Yet until the early 1600s few farmhouses had a separate kitchen, the hall serving this purpose.

Other men's flowers always smell sweeter . . . Flower gardens are of very ancient origin, exemplified by the famous Hanging Gardens of Babylon, one of the Seven Wonders of the World.

In 1872, in a letter to *The Times* that made his name, Richard Jefferies reported that the average common day-labourer received in cash wages about twelve shillings a week. The modern farmworker still struggles to gain parity with factory workers who make far more money for far fewer hours.

A hundred years ago, agricultural workers numbered well over a million. Nowadays, those numbers have declined many times, yet farming is still our largest industry.

The basket-maker's is one of the most ancient of crafts. Even before he established a settled home, the basket-maker needed something in which to gather the wild fruits or the sea-food he depended on.

Before the clipping machine, sheepshearing, like so much other farmwork, was the occasion for a festival. Shakespeare's contemporary, Michael Drayton, described how the bagpipes played in celebration and the shearers feasted on syllabubs, curds, 'clouted' cream, and other country dainties.

Only after the mid-sixteenth century did the public house require a licence. Anyone selling ale simply hung out on a pole the traditional 'bush', a bunch of ivy and vine leaves — the first inn signs — hence the expression 'Good wine needs no bush'.

RIGHT
The representatives of the middle class in the village today are mainly commuters or people who have retired to the countryside. But in the period between the reign of Elizabeth I and the Restoration, the number of small gentry and yeoman freeholders was on the increase.

If she is going to the village flower show, she should be awarded first prize for ingenuity.

It is good that we do not always take the 'kindly fruits of the earth' for granted and sometimes pay tribute to them.

Look upon this picture and on that, as we might say. Life during the old man's youth was infinitely harder. Apart from the conditions in which he lived and worked, he probably received a wage of thirty shillings a week — less than an evening's beer-money for a modern youth, even allowing for the adjustment in present-day terms. A motorcar, even a motorbike, was out of the question for the old man, and his whole life was far more intimately bound up with his native village

In the fourteenth century John de Trevisa wrote: 'The catte is best in youth, swift, pliant, and merry, and leapeth and rusheth on all things that is before him. He is a right heavy beast in age, and full sleepy, and lieth slily in wait for mice.'

Byron would not have believed it: an English summer day as hot and calm as this evidently is. And what could be more villagy – especially if the beer is good.

Confident that the day was theirs, Reg and Alf had complacently trotted only a single, but all at once Alf realized that the ball wasn't going to carry. The spectators groaned, too, as they also realized that the ball was going to land a few paces inside the boundary. It would most likely bounce over for four, and we would be pipped.

Certainly the ball landed, but it didn't bounce. It just stayed strangely put as the Great Noshington curate pranced towards it. Meanwhile, in desperation, Alf and Reg had started running again. Once, twice, three times they crossed. . .

'Quick! Throw the ruddy thing in!' bawled the visitor's captain, as the curate inexplicably hesitated, positively dancing around the ball with fluttering hands as if he had come across a Mills bomb instead of a cricket ball.

'Run!' equally bawled Reg, and we could hear the batsmen panting as they charged to and fro. Four! Five! . . . SIX! — all run — for the ball had landed in an immense cow-pat and before another of the Great Noshington fielders, made of sterner stuff than the curate, had fished it out, Alf and Reg had made certain of victory. Those errant heifers of Mr Bernstein's had won the match for us.

Trivial? On the contrary. For generations village cricket has been a binding social cement that has been of profound importance for the tolerance which was for so long the hall-mark of our society, whatever blemishes may appear from time to time. Cricket — village cricket, one emphasizes — has been even more democratic than our voting system, which does, after all, preclude peers and lunatics. After quoting a match in 1747 in which the captain of the Kent XI was the gardener at Knole and Lord John Sackville a member of his team, G.M. Trevelyan went on to say that 'If the French noblesse had been capable of playing cricket with their peasants, their châteaux would never have been burnt.'

'And of course, dear boy,' said the Brigadier, sipping his Guinness that evening in The Lamb as we celebrated that famous victory, 'if the French themselves had played cricket at all, the world would have been a different place. Only let them comprehend the rules of cricket and the *Entente* really would be *cordiale*! I tell you what! You know Fleckham is twinned with that town in Normandy? Why don't they teach their twin how to play cricket and have an annual match? Marvellous idea, eh? Why, look how civilized the Danes and the Dutch are — and they play cricket.'

It is astonishing and perhaps significant how many authors in the past have been fascinated by village cricket. There was the famous match in *Pickwick Papers* when Podder and Dumkins performed such heroic feats for All-Muggleton, 'blocking the doubtful balls, missing the bad ones, taking the good ones, and sending them flying to all parts of the field' with such devastating force that Dingley Dell were thrashed, in spite of all the efforts of the eager Luffey and the enthusiastic Struggles. And the splendid flower show match Siegfried Sassoon played in as a schoolboy (described in *Memoirs of a Fox-hunting Man*), when the home team's umpire 'was accused of making holes in the pitch with his wooden leg in order to facilitate the efforts of their bowlers'. There was, too, the unforgettable match in which A.G. Macdonnell poked gentle fun at this very English game, little knowing that the day would come when the England Test team would be successively captained by a Welshman and a Scotsman.

But the most surprising devotee of village cricket was Mary Mitford who, in the days of George IV, was positively excited by it, especially by

> a real solid old-fashioned match between neighbouring parishes, where each attacks the other for honour and a supper, glory and half a crown a man. If there

> be any gentlemen amongst them, it is well — if not, it is so much the better. Your gentleman cricketer is in general rather an anomalous character. Elderly gentlemen are obviously good for nothing; and young beaux are, for the most part, hampered and tramelled by dress and habit: the stiff cravat, the pinched-in waist, the dandy-walk — oh, they will never do for cricket! Now, our country lads, accustomed to the flail or the hammer (your blacksmiths are capital hitters), have the free use of their arms; they know how to move their shoulders; and they can move their feet too — they can run; then they are so much better made, so much more athletic, and yet so much lissomer.

She would have been delighted, but not surprised, to know that renowned English cricketers such as 'Farmer' White and Harold Gimblett had started their careers in village cricket!

SEPTEMBER

Although nothing can supplant the importance of the annual cricket match against Great Noshington, and the fervour it arouses among many of the villagers, the Flower Show (which embraces many other activities than its title implies) not only brings in far more people but also arouses a fervour of a different kind. To begin with, the holding of a flower show at all was for long a matter of controversy, jealousy, even rancour, for although William Hazlitt was not always perfectly fair towards country people in calling them stupid for want of thought, and selfish for want of society, he was perfectly right in saying that (at times) they hated each other. This, of course, is all part of the fact that, as we have mentioned before, country life is far less anonymous than in the town, where you tend to hate institutions rather than individuals.

Anyway, for a number of years as far as the Flower Show was concerned, it was a question not of one pope, nor even two — the schism ran deeper than that: there were three popes, in a horticultural sense. The Women's Institute ran their own flower show, together with such items as knit-wear, soft toys, breadmaking and so on. The Village Hall Committee, stimulated by one of those periodical feuds, ran their show — all this brought about by village politics, the wife of the then chairman of the Village Hall Committee having been ousted from her presidency of the WI. And the third show, a fairly select and dignified affair, was mounted by the Garden Club.

Needless to say, there was much overlapping as far as personnel were concerned, but the Garden Club consisted largely of, as they put it, the more serious gardeners. They hold quizzes, invite speakers, organize visits to well-known gardens, while the highlight of the Club's career was many years ago, in the early days of *Gardener's Question-time*, when the BBC and their horticultural pontiffs did a programme in the village hall. In addition, the Garden Club, by ordering in bulk, is able to get more advantageous terms for its members, who put in for their requirements at the annual meeting.

Well, now, it was not long before it became apparent to the saner members of our community that it was plain daft for the village to hold three different shows. It not only created ill-feeling, but it dissipated effort. So, on the initiative of the Rector and the Squire's wife, a village meeting was called, the upshot of which was that a Village Flower Show Committee was formed, with representatives from all the bodies concerned, plus a leavening of co-opted neutral members.

As a result, our annual Flower Show is a much larger affair, and indeed an impressive one. It is surprising what a small village can produce — what hidden talents are revealed as one strolls around the tables that are laden with exhibits. Professional-looking walnut cakes, layer cakes, bottles of home-made wine of splendid Tyrrhenian purple, handsome, scrumptiously nutty crusted wholemeal loaves that make one wonder how that dreadful pre-sliced white bread can ever find a market — and, my word, what is this? The red card of victory propped against one of those same sturdy loaves: first prize for a wholemeal loaf ('must be baked the previous day') to Captain RN! One glances round at him in even greater awe as, hands thrust in jacket pockets, with thumbs thrust out confidently — like a portrait of Beatty — he chats to the Rector's wife who is to declare the show open.

Moving further along the tables, jostling among the other villagers — and quite a few Great Noshington folk — we come to the produce section: strawberry jam, raspberry jam, pickled walnuts, pickled onions, lemon curd, Bakewell tarts — and, yes, of course, what would you expect? — first prize to Mrs Bragham! After all, she's been making Bakewell tarts all her life — Coketown, it's in that area, so perhaps she had an advantage. There's a photographic section and the slightly embarrassed Squire has walked away with first prize by virtue of a coloured shot of a heron beadily contemplating the depths of the Drover's Pond.

There are paintings, too, with several of the village ladies turning in work that varies from unconsciously mock-Oskar Kokoschka to water-colours bringing to mind the age of Mrs Gaskell. But the best of that section by far is a charcoal sketch of his wife by the alternative economy ex-stockbroker's clerk from Nut-tree Corner who has come here to seek the good life.

All these efforts are peered at, breathed over, and generally admired or criticized by the village, shuffling *en masse* around the trestle tables. But the real heart of the show is, of course, the garden produce. The floral arrangements are accorded tolerant words of praise, but are not really considered to be serious or practical by the villagers, especially village gardeners such as that prototype Jim Fallow. The flowers themselves — the dahlias, gladiolas, asters, and so on — they matter all right, but it is the vegetables above all that bring to the collective eye a glint of interest, jealousy, and even suspicion. Fat lettuces big as cabbages (how on earth, I wonder, thinking of my own yellowing all-the-year-rounds whose hearts will scarcely give shelter to a couple of slugs, how on earth do people grow such beauties?); parsnips, already!, runner-beans — but they must be tough, that length — they ought to judge vegetables by their flavoursomeness, not just for size; bunches of parsley — mine is going to seed already; carrots big as wedges; beetroot like cannonballs. What toil and care and skill have gone into it all. The villagers really have, as we have said before, worshipped the soil.

And vegetable marrows — enormous, self-satisfied looking creatures.

'How du Joe Pickup grow 'em like that? Why, they marrows would poke through his fence on to the village street, his garden's so small's a pocket hankercher. Here, Joe, have you read the rules?'

'What rules, then?'

'The one that says all exhibits in section one, three, four and five *must* have been produced by the exhibitor. Tell us who's your greengrocer?'

Joe's response is unprintable, as he shoulders his way through the crowd, and also inaudible, which is just as well, for the Rector's wife is about to declare the show officially open.

I am sure Joe is innocent (after all, he *is* treasurer of the village hall) and that he deserves his first prize for those gargantuan marrows. But it is a fact that an extraordinary amount of cheating does go on at shows everywhere — it hasn't changed since the days of Siegfried Sassoon's flower show: 'such a dreadful thing, the judges have found out that Bathwick has been cheating with his prize vegetables — He bought all his vegetables in Ashbridge. The judges suspected him, so they went to his garden in a pony trap and found that he has *no glass* — not even a cucumber frame!'

But let us thread our way through the crowd and have a cream tea, by courtesy of the WI, then go across the road, for the 'sports' are starting in Rooky Wood Meadow (by kind permission of Mr Albert Dunch). The three-legged race, the sack race — yes, they still go on; the hoop-la; the coconut shy (actually we find it more expedient to use empty beer-cans as the target); the fortune-teller in her tent, looking like a real-life Romany, but suspected of being Mrs Slee; the greasy pole and pillow fight, in which, to warm things up, Mr Maundy-Hansom and Jeremy Dredge stage a spectacular contest; the races in which it seems all the fat little boys of the entire county are taking part, guessing the weight of a pigling (presented by G. Hussey Esq.); a display by the Fleckham Pony Club, of which various village children are members; while during the afternoon, at suitable intervals, the Fleckham Silver Band shatters the autumnal air with renderings of 'The Little Ploughboy' and 'Hearts of Oak'.

None of these bucolic jollities, however, can compete in popular acclaim with the great train race, which was obviously invented by a male chauvinist, for it entails the womenfolk of the village, including such as Gertie Slocum, Mrs

Endacott, young Mrs Slee, even Black-eyed Susie, taking part in an event which has us alternately cheering ourselves hoarse and splitting our sides, as the saying is. For each competitor there is a suitcase, full of old clothes, and of course the more freakish these are, the better. The women have to race fifty yards, open their respective suitcases, put on the garments inside, race back again to the starting-post, take off the clothes and repack them in the suitcases. . .

You sneer with Hazlitt? We are unmoved. Trivial our rustic caperings may seem; we enjoy them, nevertheless.

That evening, when I went round to Captain RN for a drink, he showed me a brown-stained programme of rural sports held in 1797 at Maiden Castle, in Dorset. It read like this:

1 To be played for at cricket, a round of beef.
2 A cheese to be rolled down the hill. Prize to whoever stops it.
3 A silver cup to be run for by ponies — best of three heats.
4 A pound of tobacco to be grinned for.
5 A barrel of beer to be rolled down the hill. Prize to whoever stops it.
6 A Michaelmas goose to be dived for.
7 A good hat to be cudgelled for.
8 A half-guinea for the best ass — in three heats.
9 A handsome hat for the boy most expert in catching a roll dipped in treacle, and suspended by a string.
10 A leg of mutton and a gallon of porter to the winner of a race of 100 yards in sacks.
11 A good hat to be wrestled for.
12 Half-a-guinea to the rider of the ass who wins the best of three heats, by coming in last.
13 A Pig. Prize to whoever catches him by the tail.

'Makes our sports seem a bit tame, don't you think?' said Captain RN as he drank his gin.

Gone, more's the pity, are the days of the harvest home, when, according to Thomas Tusser (in his sixteenth-century *500 Points of Good Husbandrie*)

In harvest time, folks, servants and all,
Should make all together good cheere in their hall;
And fill out the black boule of bleith to their song,
And let them be merie all harvest time long.

Once ended thy harvest, let none be beguilde,
Please pay such as did helpe thee, man, woman, and childe.
Thus dooing, with alway such helpe as they can,
Thou winnest the praise of the labouring man.

In far off days, in Sam Dredge's childhood, and certainly in his father's time, the harvest was still truly the crown of the year, when men, aware in the hidden depths of their being of the struggle humanity has always had to wage in order to gain its daily bread, gave expression in heartfelt fashion to their joy and relief that another year's wheat, the real staff of life, had been successfully garnered in. No wonder they rejoiced. They elected a harvest queen, and brought her home in triumph, clad in immaculate white and carrying in her arms the last sheaf, decorated with ribbons and flowers, as she sat on top of the laden wagon; the

In the biblical phrase, the Judge of 'all the earth' can be relied upon to do right; but judges at a flower-show are certain to be criticized by all but the winners.

It is to be hoped potential customers at this village 'do' are not being deterred by the watchdog, or all those good home-made stuffs will go soggy in the summer sun.

In *An English Farmhouse*, Geoffrey Grigson said that no other form of roofing makes life underneath it so pleasant as thatch does. The saying that it is cool in summer and warm in winter may be a platitude, but it is eminently true. Even with our modern methods and materials, we have evolved nothing as effective.

The thatched cottage is often looked upon as the prototype English village home, but in fact it is really only found in southern England. In face of all the changes that have taken place in the countryside, thatching remains one of the few crafts that cannot be mechanized.

narrow hedges plucked tribute from the golden load. And by dint of the harvest supper afterwards, the farmer made some small recompense — conscience-money, some called it — to his labourers, whose pay and conditions in those days were indeed abominable.

> The barn's floor was cleared, and a long table of boards and tresells reached almost from door to door. Not only the regular labourers and their wives but all who occasionally worked on the farm were invited. On their arrival a depression seemed to rest upon the company. Self-conscious, in their best on a working-day, they stood in groups, scarcely daring to open their mouths. In spite of a huge crimson dahlia in his button-hole, young John Brook, the assistant sexton, appeared to mistake the nature of the solemnity. Carter and Shepherd gazed dumbstruck on the white tablecloth. Their wives attentively considered the chestnut rafters of the barn's roof to assure themselves that they were at ease. Selina Jane called for room to pass with the beef, and the spell was broken. Every tongue was loosed. One and all bustled into their places and it was necessary to hammer many times with the handle of the carving-knife before silence could be obtained for the saying of Grace.*

Well, all that is gone, swallowed up in the maw of the combine harvester. But we still have our Harvest Festival, we are still aware of what we owe to the earth, and the church is now a veritable temple to the glory of Ceres. Some of those same splendid striped marrows huddle at the foot of the pulpit, like a litter of strange wild piglings fallen asleep through overeating. Strings of onions hang from the lectern (it is to be hoped they don't draw tears from whoever reads the lesson). Sheaves of wheat from Town Farm are propped against some of the

*W. Raymond, *The English Country Life* (1910)

pillars. Fat plums lie opulently in their baskets. An open half-sack of apples vie in colour with sleek tomatoes on a willow pattern dish. Jars of honey glint on a bench, for we have several beekeepers in the village. (Mr Scales sells their surplus in the village shop.) Grapes from the Brigadier's greenhouse keep company with Jim Fallow's cannonball cabbages which are round and hard enough to be used on a bowling-green. And everywhere flowers — dahlias, michaelmas daisies, late roses — and all of these, flowers, vegetables, fruit and wheat putting forth an earthy perfume — aroma, odour, tang, call it what you will — of far greater significance than any incense.

And into the church, like some tiny messenger sent by Ceres to make sure our tribute is worthy enough, wanders a bumble-bee, which goes from offering to offering, sampling each in turn.

After the service Mr Bragham could be heard in earnest conversation with Robert Brimblecombe who is people's warden. Do you think, Mr Brimblecombe (Mr Bragham is a great stickler for protocol), do you think it would be a pleasant idea if we could revive the old custom of the harvest supper . . . ?

He really couldn't miss an opportunity like that and I wouldn't mind betting that by next year he has persuaded the Rector and the Church Council.

Of course, it is always a profound satisfaction to gather baskets of produce from your own garden — peas that lie so incredibly neat and shiny in the pod, plump strawberries, most opulent of fruit, runner-beans which the more you pick them the more they put forth, the buried treasure of potatoes, beautifully clean in a good year and always the odd one or two trying to remain concealed until you grub them out with your hand groping in the summer-warmed soil — and a triumph to have succeeded in something fairly unusual such as celeriac or kohl rabi.

Yet there is a different, special satisfaction about gathering the wild fruits of the earth. Is it the innate gratification of something for nothing, or man's arrogant wonder that these 'kindly fruits of the earth' can be put forth without any effort on his part — no digging, no planting or sowing, no hoeing or pruning? Or is it something atavistic within us, unconsciously remembering far-distant times when we had only those wild fruits to depend on? Or is it the simple thrill of seeking and finding?

Mushrooms come high on the list — not simply the conventional field or horse mushrooms, welcome though these are, and some fields in the parish positively snow with them, but also some of the Boletus family such as the nutty blusher, so called because it turns pink when peeled, or the lovely yellow chanterelle with its delicate apricot fragrance; and many others from the beef-steak mushroom to the uncommon blewits, and so many more that are edible if you take care to know them. Even puff-balls can be tastily fried.

The villagers steer clear of such exotics, and on one occasion when my wife and I had the Captain RN to a meal, he put down his knife and fork with grim finality on discovering there were 'toadstools' in the ragout. He had been through shot and shell, fought at Matapan, pursued the *Bismarck*, but those highfalutin fungi were a hazard he was not prepared to face. No guest of the Borgias could have spent a night more racked with unease than did that gallant officer.

If you search earnestly enough some of our banks are minutely studded with wild strawberries, tiny, too fiddling for many people to bother about, but their flavour is exquisite and they must of a surety have featured on the menu in Titania's days. Blackberry-gathering has come back again (blackberries went out

'Nothing to eat but food . . . '

'But for these vile guns', to borrow Hotspur's words from another context, the English countryside would have been a pleasanter and a richer place. They created an atmosphere more bitter than the reek of saltpetre itself.

of favour somewhat when sugar was rationed), and blackberry and apple pie, with dollops of cream, is sheer gastronomic ecstasy! Crab-apples, delightful miniatures, come only rarely, but when they do they produce a jelly of a superb colour. And a jelly — for meat, that is, if you haven't any red currants — can be made from the glorious jewels of the rowan, which rarely fail. It has a rather bitter flavour, but you can mitigate this by mixing rowan berries with apple.

Sloes, too, with their marvellous blue bloom, come in useful (especially after the first frosts have taken the edge off their sourness), and I could mention a certain maiden lady in the village who makes a most potable sloe-gin, which, after she has put it away — lost it, she terms it — for a year or two, turns out a fine purple. She would never dream of indulging in gin on its own, but has convinced herself that sloes make it genteelly admissible. She is very careful to make sure it is properly drinkable, which naturally entails some expert tasting — but then, her glasses are very small . . .

That is a digression. One of the wild specialities of the village is hazelnuts (not for nothing is Nut-tree Corner so called). We have two or three copses famous for them, and the villagers, women and children especially, keep a watchful eye on each other to avoid their rivals stealing a march. The result is that very often the nuts are gathered before they are properly ripe — although to a certain extent they will ripen afterwards.

There are wild nutters, too. At night, that most charming but rarely seen character the dormouse, large eyed and bushy tailed, climbs among the branches and makes the neatest holes in the shells, just big enough to extract the kernel. Frequently, scattered on the moss beneath the trees, there is evidence of his feasting — which helps him to grow fat for his winter sleep. The squirrel, too — alas, the ubiquitous grey American, brought to this country a hundred years ago — profits from them, but forgets many of the nuts he stores up, for you can often find them next spring concealed in some mossy cache.

Even though the best nutting entails trespassing, some of us like to think certain stretches of woodland are our own private domain, and if people are forestalled in this way, black looks tend to be exchanged — regardless of the fact that the property in question actually belongs to the Squire or Farmer Slocum or George Hussey. But chagrin is mutual if any gypsies happen to be in the neighbourhood at the time and have the gross impertinence to appear at village doors or in the market-town offering baskets of hazelnuts — bigger than any we ever seem to find.

Everyone through the ages has enjoyed nutting, for there is something childishly attractive about the neat brown shells (was it not Queen Mab whose chariot, an empty hazelnut, was drawn by a team of 'little atomies'?) while nothing can compare with the solid 'meat' of the hazelnut and its peculiar, particular sweetness.

John Clare used to enjoy nutting:

> The rural occupations of the year
> Are each a fitting theme for pastoral song
> And pleasing in our autumn paths appear
> The groups of nutters as they chat along
> The woodland rides . . .

OCTOBER

There are several farmers in the parish, from the Squire himself with his Home Farm and his Dexters, to the young newcomer who has just taken on George Thornback's place and is bristling with agricultural college ideas, and whose fond papa has provided him with the wherewithal to invest in an array of ultra-modern machinery out of all proportion to that modest property. 'Might try my hand at some contract-work,' he explains uneasily, as somebody comments wryly on it in The Lamb. And Harry Biggin is not best pleased at that, for he already does the rounds at ploughing and harvest times, many farmers finding it more convenient to have the heavy work done for them rather than keep too much expensive machinery that otherwise is used only occasionally.

But it is Mr Slocum in the village itself who is the real bucolic prototype. With his bluff kindliness and never-failing good humour, he might be one of Walter de la Mare's three jolly farmers who bet a pound each would dance the others off the ground. Even in these impersonal days when most of the old matiness has vanished from the hayfield and the last patch of corn is no longer the occasion for a miniature battue as the rabbits make a bolt for it, Mr Slocum still contrives to make one believe 'How blest beyond all blessings are farmers, if they but knew their happiness!'

His geese hiss a warning from behind the handsome new iron gates, which were made for him by Jack Farley. The supplicating noise of his hungry pigs rings out over the village. His herd of Friesians, sleek, swag-uddered matrons, still amble with dewy-eyed indifference down the village street (at least when they are grazing Lond Meadow), causing one of the new 'residents', a retired quantity surveyor from a south-coast town, to complain about the mess. The newcomer has even suggested that the Parish Council should cover over the stream to prevent the cows congregating near the post office. 'People like that,' snorts the Brigadier, 'might as well be living in a suburb. They complain about honest to goodness country muck and foul the place up with their cars!' (There are few new residents like that — most hasten, metaphorically, that is to say, to get their boots plastered with muck, as a means of being accepted.)

But the activity we most associate with Mr Slocum is his cider-making. All the year round a steady number of customers call at the farm, including an astonishing number of little old men whom you never see anywhere else and who look like earthenware pitchers themselves already filled to the brim with cider; or the Young Farmers' Club from Fleckham holding a barbecue; even Mr Bernstein turns up in his Mercedes to fetch a jar ('my gardener likes it, you know'). And several publicans come from afar, for Mr Slocum's cider, especially his Harvest Scrumpy, is good, strong, and very cheap: the distant publicans sell it at more than twice the price they pay Mr Slocum, although Jeremy Dredge knows only too well that he cannot charge too much and is thankful that many people prefer beer or spirits.

Now in October it isn't the customers with their carboys and plastic containers that draw attention to Town Farm. It is the glorious, rich, unmistakable tang that pervades the neighbourhood. For the cider-pressing season has started and, as in Sackville-West's lines:

> And all the air was sweet and shrill
> With juice of apples heaped in skips,
> Fermenting, rotten, soft with bruise,
> And all the yard was strewn with pips,
> Discarded pulp and wrung-out ooze
> That ducks with rummaging flat bill
> Searched through beside the cider-press
> To gobble in their greediness.

Counties such as Kent and Worcestershire are renowned for their fruit orchards, but Devon, Somerset and Herefordshire are the stronghold of cider or 'scrumpy'. Worcestershire pears can provide perry, but this was written off by William Camden in the sixteenth century as 'a counterfeit wine, both cold and flatulent'.

One of the most satisfying aspects of gardening is that nothing need be wasted. The debris of the harvest rots down on the compost heap and helps nourish the earth for its next generous putting-forth.

Mostly it is the little green and red apples from Mr Slocum's own orchard, but farmers from ten miles away bring theirs in, too, during the next two or three months, for the season will last until after Christmas. Day after day the great cider-house rumbles and hums as the fan-belt from the tractor works the crushing-mill. Overhead in the loft Alf tips sack after sack of apples into the hopper, where they dance and bounce as if reluctant to enter the clutches of the grinder, although Alf quells the mutiny with his dung-spattered wellingtons. And down below Mr Slocum stands by the chute through which the pulp spews, and is soon flecked with it as if by some unusual snowstorm.

When the concrete vat is full, Mr Slocum bangs on the wooden beams with a shovel handle and the flow comes to a halt for the time-being. He smoothes flat the great mass of juicy pulp, which looks like some fluffy confection, and then, by the pailful, deeply covers the nylon cloths on the trolley-load of racks, folding each over its contents in a neat, large, flat parcel, while from the racks, through sheer weight, a stream of apple-juice speeds down the gutter.

When the racks are full with their slab-like loads, he pushes the trolley on its little runners into the press, switches on, and a contented, authoritative hum begins to compete with the clatter of the tractor. Slowly, barely perceptibly, the trolley rises up and the trickle of juice becomes a merry, whirling flood gushing into the underfloor tank, from which it is piped into the first of the dozens of gargantuan, comfortably recumbent casks that greyly line the cider-house, looking like some weird species of unworldly creatures with an insatiable thirst.

Up to six or seven years ago, Mr Slocum still worked a hand-press, using wadges of straw between the layers of pomace instead of nylon cloths. The resulting great cube or 'cheese', as it was called, entailed back-breaking, sinew-creaking work for two men who had to heave and push on the crank, and the more apples they could press at a time — almost a ton — the better. (Once upon a time horses were used in some cider houses.) But, apart from the labour, it had another disadvantage: the process took three days to complete, by which time the pomace was beginning to ferment, so that afterwards it couldn't be fed to the cows because the milk would be tainted. Now, however, with the much faster electric press, the pomace can be fed the same day to the cows, who love it. During the drought-year of 1976, when pasture was still yellow and bare in autumn, the pomace came in especially useful. As for the pigs, they had always been given the pomace which they fought over viciously, and if you had a tipsy sow or two they would simply sleep it off.

There had 'always' been a cider-house at Town Farm, 'leastaways', says Mr Slocum, shouts, rather, pausing to wipe pomace, pips, and rind from face and shirt, 'leastaways I know for certain-sure my granfer had one and I shoulden wonder *his* granfer afore 'un. What's more granfer did the rounds once upon a time. He was a travelling cider-maker as well as making his own.'

It was exactly as in *The Woodlanders* in which Giles Winterbourne's 'press and mill were fixed to wheels instead of being set up in a cider-house; and with a couple of horses, buckets, tubs, strainers, and an assistant or two, he wandered from place to place, drawing very satisfactory returns for his trouble in such a prolific season as the present'.

'Ah, my dear soul,' says Mr Slocum, as if echoing Hardy, 'I han't never seen such a season as this for apples. Reckon I'd have enough in a two-mile area this year. There gooing to be tons and tons of 'em will just bide rotting away in the grass.'

'Well, my friend, I promised you a bumper harvest when we did the wassailing back in January, remember?' For appropriately enough, silhouetted in the great doorway, it was Mr Bragham who had come to see the first of this year's vintage, as he called it.

'Why, so 'ee did, midear, so 'ee did!' cried Mr Slocum, appreciatively. 'Come along in, then, and try a glass of apple-juice.' And though as yet there were no beaded bubbles winking at the brim, we partook with much satisfaction of the cleanly natural, pale amber liquid which would, before very long, be transmuted into that most English and pleasantly intoxicating drink, much more potent than many an unwary tippler has realized.

I discovered by chance that Mr Slocum has a rival, in a manner of speaking — not in cider-making, but in the production of another traditional drink, although in this case it is for home consumption only and does not entail any wrestling with Customs and Excise returns.

Now, as a boy, more than half a century ago, I used to know a farmer who was an enthusiastic bee-keeper and, more to the point here, an equally enthusiastic distiller of mead, that ancient drink produced by the fermentation of honey and water. It was a beverage particularly associated with the Saxons and other Germanic folk, who had great faith in its ability to stimulate song and prophecy; in other words, they used to get drunk on it. We have been left with a mental picture of those fair-haired warriors carousing stridently and raising their drinking-horns in one interminable, thick-tongued binge, which continued, they believed, when they entered Valhalla. It is also said that the term honeymoon comes from the Teutonic custom of drinking mead for thirty days after the nuptials. (Shakespeare wouldn't have thought that a good idea, for he declared that alcohol increases the desire but diminishes the performance.)

Nowadays, mead tends to be despised as a rather folksy drink, but, like beer which can be turned into real stingo potent enough to satisfy the miller in the nursery song, you can make mead as strong as you fancy. And I can quite understand those Saxon tipplers if that old farmer's mead was anything to go by, for the golden-yellow liquor that he made was more deceptive and more alcoholic than any cider. He had one particular farming crony who would come over every so often for a game of penny nap. They would start off their evening sedately enough, sipping at their glasses — and looking rather like bees themselves, delicately thrusting their proboscides into the nectar — but little by little the point of no return would be reached. And at length, late into the night, the visitor had to be helped into his gig, whereupon the faithful pony would take its befuddled master home at a walking-pace along the dark lanes — and never once was that merry old bibber decanted into a ditch.

I was reminded of all this recently. One of our bee-keepers, Miss Flora Bundy, had asked me to take her extractor in the car to the newcomers at Nut-tree Corner, to whom she was lending it. Her own honey, and that of most other bee-keepers, had long ago been extracted, but if you don't possess an extractor yourself, you tend to be late. (Simply stated, the sections containing the honeycombs are placed upright around the centre of the machine which is then rotated at high speed by hand or, nowadays, electricity, the honey eventually being drawn off through a tap at the bottom.)

Well, as I drew up at Nut-tree Cottage, there could be heard the strumming of a guitar accompanying a baritone voice raised, somewhat surprisingly, not in one of those phoney modern folk-songs, but a genuine sea-shanty. Somebody seemed to be setting sail on Friday morn but was being delayed by espying a fair pretty maid with a comb and a glass in her hand. She couldn't have been up to any good, for no true sailor willingly goes to sea on a Friday.

The twanging of the guitar was not nearly as mellow — I think that in the

Not least of the many pagan rites absorbed and glossed over by the Church is the Harvest Festival, in thanks to God for the bounty of the earth.

Although compulsory education, as we know it, started little more than a hundred years ago, a surprising number of dame schools and charity schools existed in the eighteenth century, for man's thirst for knowledge cannot be suppressed.

circumstances 'mellifluous' could fairly be used here — as the voice. But my arrival brought a temporary halt to the raging seas that had been roaring away and there followed a faintly uneasy hiatus in which the good life couple and I felt our way among a forest of platitudes, for we had scarcely met before. Relief came, when, stroking his prophet's beard speculatively, he invited me with a deprecatory cough, to have a glass of mead.

'It's the only thing I can offer you. Except for beer. You may not think much of the mead. I made it a couple of years ago before we left our last place. Er — you won't find it too strong . . . '

'It's got to be strong to be good,' I said, hopefully rather than anxiously.

'Ah, true, very true,' and a glint came into his eyes, while his wife fetched a little pottery beaker. After hearing that voice raised in song, I was not surprised to find that the mead was both strong and good, and I enjoyed being taken back through the years — although fortunately I did not have to be taken back physically afterwards like that old farmer, for the internal combustion engine is not as sensible as a veteran pony.

The mead was a pleasant tongue-loosener, and before long I had learned how sterile life as 'something in the city' had been. No POW could have planned his escape from Colditz more keenly. It was easy to see from the frugality of the cottage that their search for the good life was far from smooth, materially at least. By far the best piece of furniture was a handsome birchwood spinning-wheel. But in other ways it seemed rich enough and I knew from reports by Miss Bundy, who befriends all creatures from fallen sparrows to struggling humans, how hard the couple worked on their small holding, living as basically as possible, not merely from necessity but from choice — keeping a pig (and soon to be faced with the wrench of killing and eating it), growing an acre of wheat, raising their own poultry, grazing their goats on the common, selling as many of their vegetables as possible through the WI stall in Fleckham, and hoping to sell some of their honey to Mr Scales.

It is an uphill task, yet strangely enough I sense among the villagers a kind of jealousy towards them, for they are only trying to be what the villagers' own ancestors once were — self-supporting. Perhaps it is that which causes the jealousy: the villagers are unconsciously reminded that they are no longer independent themselves and resent the newcomers making far more use of the Drover's Lea than they do.

Maybe if they could partake of that excellent mead, their attitude would mellow. But I guess the Nut-tree Corner home-brew would be more appropriate — and indeed is more characteristic of that lost independence — for in Cobbett's childhood (in a book about the country you cannot get away from Cobbett for long), 'to have a house and not to brew was a rare thing indeed'. He went on to lament the fact that 'the drink which has come to supply the place of beer has, in general, been tea. It is notorious that tea has no useful strength in it; that it contains nothing nutritious; that it, besides being good for nothing, has badness in it, because it is well known to produce want of sleep in many cases. No good labourer who has attained middle age, can look back upon the last thirty years of his life, without cursing the day in which tea was introduced into England!'

The search for the good life may be fraught with hardships and difficulties, but these Nut-tree Corner folk know how to bring a certain good cheer into it.

Carnival is usually associated with the rip-roaring orgy that precedes Lent, when people fortify themselves for the six-week abstinence that follows. Not so down our way. Carnival time is in October, perhaps originally an extension of harvest thanksgiving of a rowdier, secular, and more spectacular kind, when dark, hopefully mellow autumn evenings necessitate a galaxy of lights which add to the drama of the scene. Besides, there is more time, as gardens become less demanding, potatoes have been lifted, carrots stored, and bonfires of bean haulms announce the end of the growing season.

Or are these blaring, garish, torch-lit festivals a shout of defiance at the on-coming winter?

The village itself is not big enough to warrant its own carnival, so we join in the revels in other nearby parishes, especially the market-town, which is the grand culmination of it all. For weeks now, the village Carnival Committee, composed of the Amateur Dramatic Society and the Village Hall Committee, have been busy working on the float they are going to enter, and which will do the rounds in half a dozen places to make the effort worth while. It is a widespread effort, too, several of the ladies stitching away devotedly at the costumes, Mr Maundy-Hansom, the young architect who works in Fleckham, superintending the props, Mr Scales of the shop painting the scenery, Bert Ford the freelance electrician arranging the lights for the lorry on which the tableau will be staged, and of course Tom Prior the coalman standing by to drive it.

The theme they have chosen is an Indian summer, and for everyone's sake we all fervently hope we shall have one in time for the carnival, for nothing is more depressing than a wet night in which to parade the result of a great deal of work. It is especially discouraging for the members of a *tableau vivant* (what an old-fashioned phrase that sounds) who have to sit bedraggled and miserable on a trailer or a lorry while the rain lashes down. All is well this year, however — October has done us proud. The air is almost balmy with autumnal ripeness, pipistrelles still flicker around the eaves, the last flames of dahlias glow in cottage gardens — and, all expectation in the mellow evening, the village, if not *en masse*, at least in fair old numbers has loyally gone over to Great Noshington, where the first of the area carnivals is being held.

While owls hoot and the church clock strikes eight, we wait tensely on the pavements or in the gardens of friends — or strategically in the doorway of the Three Tuns — and peer impatiently into the night. Or, rather, we *listen* for the first signs of the approaching procession, for the floats have assembled and been judged at the far end of the straggling village. 'They'm coming! They'm coming!' the children cry ecstatically as the drama begins to emerge from the darkness and we can hear the stately 'pom pom tiddly om pom pom' of the Fleckham's Men's Club Silver Band, and if it was not exactly 'the most sublime noise that ever penetrated into the ear of man', it does have a nicely jolly effect and even empties (albeit very temporarily) the bar of the Three Tuns.

Then, down Church Hill, we catch sight of headlights slowly advancing, flanked by the long snaking double necklace of smaller lights on the floats themselves. With a swish of tyres a police-car slides past, putting the stamp of authority on the affair. A ragged cheer goes up as, presently, it is followed by the Marshal of the Carnival, none other than Mr Direman of the Great Noshington riding-stables, who is wearing a stetson, chaps that look as if they had been made out of a patchwork rug, and riding a grey hunter which pricks its ears and rolls a baleful eye in unease at the Silver Band pursuing it. Behind the band, and also perforce at walking-pace, comes the car bearing this year's president, one of the local doctors and his wife, who nods and waves with such regal condescension you would think her the Queen of the Carnival herself.

But the Carnival Queen is passing by now, attended on her float by her two ladies-in-waiting. She is a fat, good-natured, ginger-haired hoyden, raised to this eminent status not by her beauty but simply because it is she among the local maidens who has sold the most tickets during the previous two months. It is perhaps a safer method of choosing a queen than by some invidious beauty contest in which the judges are always suspected of favouritism. But 'pom pom pom' (how satisfying it must be to thwack that big drum, and no wonder Mr Hoggett, who plays it, has such an enormous belly — it's needed to support it) the band goes marching on, paying tribute to that frilled and flounced sovereign, smirking down on us and occasionally grabbing at her crown to keep it straight.

But it is the heart of the carnival, the floats themselves, that we are anxious to watch, for they will be in order of the places they have been awarded by the judges. Anxiously we peer . . . can it be . . . the light is too uncertain for us to tell for sure until the procession files over the little bridge . . . they're advancing at an absolute snail's pace . . . But then some of the children, perilously running up the road to meet the gaily lit convoy of lorries and trailers, come tearing back in a clatter of footsteps to yell triumphantly, 'They're first! They've won first prize!'

And now, truly, we can see for ourselves. The village has won first prize! Into the light of the houses and the street lamps the float emerges proudly, and we gaze in wonder and admiration. It is indeed an Indian summer! Alluring squaws and their children squat in front of wigwams straight out of the Wild West! Indian braves prance dramatically, somehow without advancing a single step, along the sides of the lorry, making fearsome gestures with their tomahawks, while a fearsome beast — only the churlish have any doubt that he is a buffalo — raises and lowers his woolly head, which is controlled ingeniously by a cord held by one of the braves.

And at the back of it all stands a stately Indian chief, the spit-image of Sitting Bull, bedecked in a magnificent bonnet of eagle-feathers (they could possibly be goose feathers supplied by Mrs Slocum) and a majestic cloak, while all the time he impassively draws on an enormous pipe from which issues almost more smoke than from the spluttering coal-lorry's exhaust.

And Mrs Endacott sums it all up for us.

'Oh, my!' she cries, clapping her hands ecstatically. 'Bean't it real comely! Oh, my! Woulden I like to be one of they squawses with that Mr Maundy-Hansom as chief!'

'You would have to be the chief squaw, Mrs Endacott,' says the Rector, who has joined us.

'Ah, willingly, sir, willingly! I rather fancies he,' says Mrs Endacott, with rustic frankness, and moves on down the street clutching hold of her children to enjoy the Indian summer as long as possible.

Needless to say, after the village's winning entry, the rest of the floats are somewhat of an anti-climax and we view them with critical disdain. Most of them, it seems, were based on well-known television programmes, some with a subtlety that would make it difficult to identify them, were it not for their titles in huge letters. But we must not fall into the trap of complacency because we have won first prize in the Great Noshington carnival. The real test will be at Fleckham, the biggest carnival of all: there'll be umpteen floats; no fewer than four silver bands; there'll be a fair with swings and roundabouts; a grand torchlight procession; and of course the famous blazing tar barrels that will be dragged on sleds through the town to ward off evil spirits.

NOVEMBER

What was this? Half past ten on a Saturday morning and Mrs Dredge looking exceedingly grand in a gaudy print blouse, much too flimsy for the season but that it was topped by a bulky cardigan, over which rippled a flowery apron. Jeremy, too, was all polished up, hair slicked down and wearing a tie and, believe it or not, a real old-fashioned waistcoat, while Black-eyed Susie was if possible neater and more fetching than ever.

Then I remembered. The hunt was meeting at The Lamb. I had seen the Brigadier the other day consulting the hunt-card for future reference for when his son came home on leave from Germany. And before long the meet began to take shape. There was the clip-clop of hooves as some of the local followers hacked over; one or two neighbouring farmers massive in tweeds or belted trench coats; Mr Slocum with a bowler jammed hard down over his prominent ears as if he was well aware that the hedges are tall around here; the Fleckham doctor looking as if he had prescribed himself just the right tonic; Percy Shaddock of Otterholt looking disturbingly like a fox himself (it's odd how often people resemble the creatures they hunt or shoot); the Squire's niece coolly immaculate in white stock and sleek broadcloth.

Then came the horse-boxes and the Land-Rovers and soon the flap of a cattle-truck was lowered and down the ramp poured the hounds, sterns waving joyfully, searching for the best piece of village green to foul, while a volley of whipcracks split the air as Gerry Manston the huntsman and his whipper-in instilled order into the canine riot. It goes without saying, of course, that PC Keane was on hand if need be (the banns are going to be read next Sunday). The Rector in his cassock found it necessary to loiter at the church-gate, no doubt to confer with the sexton. Miss Jekyll passed by on her way to the village shop, doubly bleak, for not only does she disapprove of hunting, but is embarrassed by the fact that the Master, a solicitor from Dumpleton, is her cousin. He politely tips his cap at her but is ignored.

Now Susie is bashfully taking out a stirrup-cup to the Master, and Jeremy, too, is plying the right people — including the Brigadier, who resembles some kind of human derrick, he towers so high on his chestnut, almost as if they had come floating in on the mist that still hangs about the chimney-stacks, for most people don't light their fires until the afternoon.

The assembled village boys (how many there seem when you encounter them in a gaggle on such an occasion) stare up at him, nudging each other and weakly tittering, and yet palpably stricken with awe and wonder. So must the wretched Aztecs long ago have gazed when first they set eyes upon the mounted Conquistadores, while it is little wonder that the Ancient Greeks made a god of the Centaur, half man, half horse, for it was a revolutionary moment in human history when man first learnt to subdue and then to ride the horse. There is still some primitive kind of inferiority at the sight of a mounted man.

Now the noise of impending drama is rising. Voices echo about the village green as if tangible, visible words are being flung to and fro between the houses on either side. Some of the hounds throw their tongues or yawn gapingly, shivering with excitement. Horses whinny, snort, stale, foam-slimy bits champ, leather creaks. 'Stand still, damn you!' 'I say, you know, you ought to have a red ribbon on that mare of yours, she'll cripple someone if she goes on lashing out like that!'

The confusion is compounded when some insufferable little boy lets off a firecracker in the drangway of The Lamb (well, after all, it is the season, and Guy Fawkes has a longer tradition than John Peel!). Some of the horses cavort and rear, the hounds give voice hysterically, as if they thought Fawkes and Fox synonymous, and the puerile pack starts up its own private chase after the culprit who, judging by the bedlam, has got himself trapped in a cul-de-sac.

Discipline among riders to hounds used to be a constant problem. 'The rush of horsemen at starting is little less than awful,' complained Surtees. 'Many a day's sport is spoilt by the sole circumstances of hounds being over-ridden.' You can tell the hunt in this picture isn't the Quorn or the Pytchley from the look of the mounts alone.

Meanwhile, Master and huntsman have been conferring earnestly with a gnomelike little man on foot, who looks as if he has only recently emerged from one of the fox-earths he has stopped during the previous night. The solicitor nods decisively, straightens up in the saddle. 'Pyet Copse, then, Gerry!' A horn twangs peremptorily, the hounds warble appreciatively, hooves clatter . . .

'They're moving off!' the cry goes up and the small boys leave their human victim and go whooping and stumbling and jostling across the green and down Market Lane, knowing full well that wherever the hunt draws they would have to start off that way.

Off goes the cavalcade, the Master in his plum-coloured coat, which once upon a time had been scarlet, stretching at the seams like an old cask which you would almost expect to see leaking (tawny port, no doubt), followed by thirty couple of ecstatic hounds looking so innocent they might be going on a school treat, the hunt 'servants', the motley field, and then the convoy of cars and Land-Rovers and bicycles and pedestrians, including inevitably, Sam Dredge. It will be he who, that evening in The Lamb, recounts every detail of the day's action for the benefit of those who have not followed the hunt.

I regret that Sam cannot read, or rather, shall we say, doesn't hold with reading, for he would certainly appreciate Surtees and all his hard-riding heroes in *Handley Cross*:

> 'Gone away!' cried Michael, 'gone away! Tally-ho! tally-ho! tally-ho! tally-ho!'
> 'Get away, hounds! get away!' holloaed Peter, cracking his whip as he trotted

The potato was cultivated in Peru and Chile long before the Spaniards brought it to Europe. Nowadays it can be an immensely prolific crop, producing as many as 20 tons an acre in favourable conditions.

> down the steep hill; and putting his bay mare straight at the fence at the bottom, went crashing through it, with a noise that resembled the outbursting of a fire in a strawyard. Then came the rush: the black threw the stone wall behind him, as a girl would her skipping rope; and James Fairlamb's cob came floundering after, bringing down the coping stones, with a rattle and clatter that would have been awful if hounds had not been running. The third man was the doctor on the dun, who made it still lower; and after him came Peter Jewitt and John Jones (the latter leading over), and impeding the progress of John Thomas, the other Jewitt, the other Jones, Morgan Hains, the overseer, and the parish-clerk of Welford, who all kept holloaing and swearing away — as obstructed gentlemen in a hurry generally do. The foot-people, seeing how hopeless was the case, stood upon the hills, lost in mute astonishment, eyeing the master on his black, careering over the meadows and hedges in a straight line with the pack, followed by the huntsman on his bay, and Fairlamb on his cob, until the scarlet coat of the latter assumed the hue of the others, and hounds, horses, and men grew
>
> Small by degrees and beautifully less.

But not to Sam. He would be in at the kill, while the Master stood 'with his fox grinning in grim death in one hand and his low-crowned hat in the other, whooping and holloaing old Bonnybell and the pack up to him'.

What is it about the hunt that so often stirs people, often into almost a frenzy of excitement, that sends even the foot-people helter-skelter in usually vain pursuit of the chase? Is it the shadowy hunter that dwells deep within us all? Is it the

Together with church and pub, the shop is one of the centres of village life, although it is under constant pressure from the supermarket. Where the local grocery store is combined with the post office, it has more chance of survival.

Before soap became readily obtainable, country folk collected the wood ash from their fires to use as a kind of lessive

historic drama of the horse, whose 'trampling feet' were man's theme tune through the centuries? Or is it sheer blood-lust, with the wretched fox helping to work off some of our complexes? All very odd. And Mrs Smart, for instance, who still rides side-saddle, is never far from the van, tally-ho's with the best of them, and was first 'blooded' fifty years ago; yet at the sight of a mouse she screams pathetically or practically goes into mourning over a young song-thrush that has broken its neck against her conservatory.

It is often imagined that fox-hunting is an age-old English tradition. In fact, its history is comparatively short. Up to the time of the Civil War in the seventeenth century, deer-hunting was the aristocratic sport. But then, many noble estates were broken up, and many deer were slain by warring soldiery or rebellious peasantry. Presently, packs of harriers were established by the squirearchy, while farmers had to content themselves with hare-coursing. Fox-hunting really only began to come into its own in the middle of the eighteenth century and even then it was for a long time a far less spectacular headlong affair than Trollope's 'fast run of forty-five minutes, almost without a check, and with a kill in the open' (that's to say, as opposed to digging out the fox). For many years hounds were bred solely for their 'nose', not for speed, and the same packs were used for hunting the hare — and the hare being comparatively local in its habits, speed was not the first requirement, but a good flair was. What is more, such packs were cheap to maintain. Somebody reckoned it cost 'less than two bottles of wine a day with their inseparable concomitants'. Even at the outset of Queen Victoria's reign, a sporting magazine could list nearly 140 packs of harriers compared with 100 packs of fox-hounds.

But when harriers began to be used increasingly for hunting foxes, this lack of speed was a great handicap. Unless the pack came upon a well-fed animal at crack of dawn, immediately after his night's foray, they were lost, for a fox put up later in the day would easily outpace the hounds. This was the reason why, in the initial days of fox-hunting, the meet would take place at a very early hour.

It was only when pioneers such as Hugo Meynell of Quorn fame bred hounds for speed and nose that fox-hunting became what E.W. Bovill called 'the most exhilarating of all field sports'. That the whole tempo did change is shown by the fact that in 1828 *The Sportsman's Directory* advised the rider to dismount at a big fence, because 'dashing at difficult leaps is merely a proof of thoughtless hardihood'.

Of course, fox-hunting — any kind of hunting — is an emotive subject and many people sincerely deplore, and actively oppose it; but it has to be said that most of them are town-dwellers. The villager or countryman in general would echo William Cobbett's growling defence of blood-sports — although possibly not for all the reasons he postulates: 'I prefer them to all other pastimes, because they produce *early rising*; and because they have no tendency to lead young men into vicious habits. It is only where men congregate that the vices haunt.'

As Cobbett said: 'The great business of life, in the country appertains, in some way or other, to the *game*, and especially at this time of year.' He was, in fact, referring to those same blood-sports he commended (but he thought 'shooters' a disagreeable class and would certainly have abominated our syndicate), although you might have imagined that he was referring to football. Indeed, some people would consider this, too, a blood-sport, judging by the horrific incidents that take place every winter Saturday all over the country. This, though, is not to be wondered at when you remember that football is the sublimation of the erstwhile

Gypsies once provided much of the casual labour
for crops such as potatoes, but machines have now largely made them redundant.
The villager always tended to be somewhat hostile to the
'travellers', perhaps subconsciously resenting their freedom, but
also anxious for his chicken run.

Guy Fawkes' Night continues to be a ritual long after the *raison d'être* has been forgotten. The occasion is partly a manifestation of man's never-ceasing fascination at the strange phenomenon of fire.

tribal affray, when our ancestors at last came to realize how counter-productive (as we might say) mutual slaughter was.

So instead of neighbouring clans and factions going to war against each other, they invented a sort of dismounted *buzkashi*, and in place of the gruesome carcass of sheep or goat or calf, favoured by the Afghans and always liable to explode unpleasantly, they used variously a bladder, a bundle of leather, even a treasured trophy plated with silver — according to the Elizabethan writer William Carew. And in this original form of soccer they could go anywhere: 'over hills, dales, and ditches. Yea, and through bushes, briars, mires, plashes and rivers.' Moreover, you could butt or pinch your opponent — a tradition that continues — while if you were in difficulties you could throw the 'ball' into the nearest bush until reinforcements came up — which surely has its modern equivalent in booting the ball into touch in moments of crisis (which evokes cries of 'Windy!' from the village boys).

That same afternoon when some folk were providing evidence of what Dickens described as the passion for hunting something that is deeply implanted in the human breast, another section of the village was partaking in this nicely contrasting activity — nicely contrasting not only in the form it takes but also because of the very different individual villagers it involves.

But to begin with the pitch: the Squire, as we have seen, entertains the Cricket Club on one of his Home Farm paddocks; the Football Club has to be content with a field on Town Farm so notoriously uneven and tussocky that it could be taken for a relic of ridge and furrow ploughing. The village has no recreation ground, although this is one of the cherished projects of Mr Deedes, the Parish Council chairman, who is constantly soliciting the local MP for help and writes frequent letters to the Playing Field Association.

The football team itself provides a nice contrast. It goes without saying that none of the 'unspeakable' who go in pursuit of the 'uneatable' ever attend a village football match, let alone play in one, while very few members of the cricket team take part — except for Alf Slocum (it is sheer coincidence that he is captain) and Dan Figgins the village postman. By and large the footballers are a different lot:

Bill Huggins, the baker's roundsman, for example, the two Farley brothers who have the seine-net franchise, Bert Budd the milk-recorder, and one of the most surprising members is the Reverend Passbody, the Methodist clergyman who visits the chapel at Bawsen Cross once a fortnight. That, too, is a nice contrast: the Church of England, in the shape of our Rector, plays cricket; the spiritual descendant of the Wesleys keeps goal for the village.

But even those members who also play cricket are almost unrecognizable on the football pitch. This is not only because of their different garb, the black and white stripes of the club giving them the nickname of the Magpies, but because the action is so much more involved. At cricket, all is leisured, only two or three players really being in motion at any one time, whereas on the relatively cramped pitch at Town Farm, it seems that all twenty-two players are in violent motion simultaneously, while the air is charged with primeval grunts and the pounding of feet more eager than skilled — an echo surely of those ancient times when the original game was a glorious excuse for a running fight that sometimes took place over miles of countryside and streets, with 'goals' in different parishes and all the local shop-keepers discreetly putting up their shutters.

Indeed, professional football — First Division, World Cup, and so on — contains far less of the real essence of the game than does village football. Artists in plenty, from Stubbs to Munnings, and not forgetting the incomparable John Leech, have depicted the hunting field, but few have turned their attention to football. One feels that Breughel (a foreigner, admittedly) would have appreciated village football especially, with all those intensely involved steaming bodies, those flaring nostrils expressive of supreme effort, cavernously gaping mouths, sweating brows and bulging veins, and with

> foot and eye opposed
> In dubious strife.

He would have seized on it all with gusto, whereas cricket, with all those frequently immobile, white-clad figures, would have appeared to him as some strange religious rite, reminiscent of the Druids.

Today's match was not of particular importance in itself, but it mattered a great deal in so far as we are in the bottom half of the County Second Division, and every point counts; the real needle match, as at cricket, is against Great Noshington. But the game now was won and lost not so much on the field but off it — to be precise behind the home goal. Once again Guy Fawkes was responsible, for at the crucial moment when the opposing centre forward (striker, I believe, in modern parlance), had felled our defence like ninepins and was feinting before delivering a blistering shot, another of those small boys let off a firecracker.

The Methodist minister was so startled that instead of being taken in by the shot, and 'going the wrong way' as it is termed, he stood rooted to the spot and the ball flashed past him into the corner of the net, to be followed within seconds by the final whistle.

Alf Whittle, father of the small boy who had set off that treacherous firework, was the most unpopular man in The Lamb that evening.

Dr Samuel Johnson said it all: 'There is nothing which has yet been contrived by man through which so much happiness is produced as by a good tavern or inn.'

G.K. Chesterton went, perhaps with tongue in cheek, so far as to ascribe the decay of democracy to the decay in the quality of the public house.

His drinking-companion Hilaire Belloc echoed him: 'When you have lost your inns drown your empty selves, for you will have lost the last of England.'

Well, all three, I am sure, would have approved of The Lamb, for it is a real 'timely inn', as Shakespeare put it, the epitome of the country pub, with its welcoming fire, its cosy settles, scrubbed tables, benches, and Windsor chairs, its faded sepia photographs on the walls, the leering fox-mask (we could do without that), and its general unspoilt rustic atmosphere which the Dredge family have had the good sense to retain, instead of turning it, as in the case of so many pubs, into something vulgarly indistinguishable from a thousand others which ring with the dreadful cacophony of the juke-box and piped music.

There isn't even a one-armed bandit to lure the villagers into emptying their pockets of loose change. The Lamb has too many other activities to occupy its regulars, quite apart from the basic occupation, for, like any proper country pub, it is by way of being a club, although you do not need to be a paid-up member to belong! And it has to be admitted that, generally speaking, it is a male club. Rarely do the village women come in, except for the likes of old Mrs Slee, who, on pension day, slips in for her favourite gin and lots of warm water and, if he doesn't get there first, tends to irritate Sam Dredge by usurping his place by the fire. When any casual visitors or holiday-makers come to the pub, the villagers tend to eye their womenfolk not exactly askance but, shall we say, with curiosity. But, then, we are faintly suspicious of any visitors, male or female.

The Lamb is not only a club, with its darts, skittles, dominoes, shove ha'penny, charity draws, running sweepstake on the first league club to score eleven goals (it has got to be the exact number), it is also the headquarters of several village activities. And it is here this evening, in the wake — the wake, indeed — of that lamentable defeat, that a meeting is held by the Football Club's Selection Committee (a grand term when you consider there are never more than thirteen or fourteen players to choose from).

Entering the pub, stern-faced men, who might be going to a Cabinet meeting, so portentous is their expression, nod briefly in answer to our greeting. They do not linger in the bar, but disappear forthwith into the 'Snug' at the back. This tiny, intimate room, reached by descending two or three steps (a hazard when you are carrying a trayful of brim-full tankards), is the headquarters of the Football Club, as it is of the Cricket Club, the Darts Committee, even of the Garden Club at times, for the Snug doesn't cost anything to hire, unlike the Village Hall Committee room which has not only to be paid for, but is bitterly cold in addition, its oil-stoves a perpetual source of controversy.

And of course Jeremy Dredge is always happy to put the Snug at the disposal of any village organization, for these earnest deliberations give rise to a gratifying thirst, and Black-eyed Susie is frequently to be seen disappearing with yet another load of bitter.

The English country pub is unique. There is nothing else like it in the world and it has fulfilled its role for countless centuries. Thatched and whitewashed, with slim, ancient bricks showing here and there through the plaster, The Lamb itself has the date 1675 carved above its lintel, and no doubt an inn existed on the spot before that. It was never a real coaching-inn, as some people like to think, but for long the local 'carrier' operated from it, fetching and carrying passengers and parcels for the coach-service that passed through the market-town. And we can be sure that those drovers we talked about earlier on called in at The Lamb, to be regaled on the liver and bacon they liked so much, to be cooked by another Mrs Dredge of a different age.

DECEMBER

The townsman has his meed of entertainment — his concerts, theatres, cinemas, first-class cricket and football, bowling greens, dance hills, bingo (saving the mark!), public tennis courts, swimming baths, greyhound tracks, speedway racing, and so on — to cater for all tastes high and low.

The villager can, of course, have access to all these if he is prepared to travel far enough — some villages are near to towns, but in our case a round journey of nearly forty miles is entailed, for the market-town has little to offer. And quite apart from the cost of those entertainments themselves, the price of petrol discourages us progressively and, as we have seen, we no longer have a railway and the bus service is virtually non-existent. Perhaps eventually village communities (especially those lucky enough to have some sort of local leadership) will perforce be thrown ever more on themselves, while chronic unemployment will, one hopes, lead to more local industries to be set up, however humble.

Of course, in a minor way, television has helped to alleviate what Lenin called the imbecility of country life — but only by introducing an imbecility of its own. And Hazlitt, too, continuing to scold (in his essay on Wordsworth's 'Excursion'), spoke scathingly of the emptiness of village life:

> There are no shops [he would not have considered Mr Scales's stores as such], no taverns, no theatres, no opera, no concerts, no pictures, no public buildings, no crowded streets, no noise of coaches or of courts of law — neither courtiers nor courtesans, no literary parties, no fashionable routs, no society, no circulating libraries, no books, or knowledge of books.

'What's the fellow going on about?' I can imagine the Brigadier snorting. 'We live in the village to avoid half the things he rails about — and the other half we do ourselves instead of having to have it laid on for us. *And* we've got the mobile library once a fortnight. Got a rattling good yarn the other day — Deighton or Innes, or something like that — every bit as good as Buchan or Rider Haggard any day!'

But whatever conditions were like in Hazlitt's day, the villager nowadays undoubtedly has far more opportunity of leisure-time activities, although in jobs like farming, quite apart from any question of inclination, the hours of work are a limiting factor. For example, cows simply have to be milked twice a day, the lambing ewes tended, the pigs fed, and the harvest brought in. And even in these days of mechanized agriculture, the farm-worker still works hours that would make a shop steward's hair stand on end, and for a wage that would make that same hair fall out.

The operative thing in all this is expressed in those suggested words of the Brigadier, '. . . and the other half we do ourselves'. Few of the people who live in the village contribute anything material to the life of the community. The only contribution the majority can make is on the social side, helping to run those astonishingly numerous activities which, harmless and bucolic as they may be and which certainly would not have satisfied Hazlitt, are at least our own: the village fête, the Flower Show, the Cricket Club, the Amateur Dramatic Society, the skittles team, the darts league, the Women's Institute, musical evenings, charity whist drives, folk dancing, the Youth Club, all the activities connected with church and chapel, and not least the Badminton Club, at which Mrs Bragham, the founder, immensely statuesque, benefits from the cunning of age to dominate a game while appearing to remain almost stationary.

(And you could at times include work in our entertainments, even on a private level. Visiting Town Farm, I found myself in what seemed to be a violent snowstorm that had broken out in the kitchen, which rang with a hubbub of festive voices. The long room was smothered in white feathers which carpeted the flagged floor, floated through the air, generously flecked the heads and shoulders of the Slocum family and their helpers, including the beshawled and desiccated Grandma Slocum who sat in the rocking-chair by the stove, her efforts constantly sabotaged by numerous cats, roused to a frenzy by this plucking session. No wonder the surviving geese out in the farmyard had been unwontedly silent: animals always know when something dire has befallen their companions. But there was nothing woe-begone about the pluckers, their work being cheered by the inevitable scrumpy Mr Slocum had brought in, while the plucking itself was made easier by the fact that Mrs Slocum had her washing-machine full of scalding water into which she dipped each bird to help loosen its feathers. And to add to the atmosphere, in came Alf Slocum, shouldering a bundle of brilliant holly, which he dumped in a corner, to the hysterical annoyance of the cats, who were lost in an explosion of feathers.)

Leaving aside that parenthetical intrusion, I was reminded of all those village activities one evening when suddenly there could be heard the crunching of many feet on the gravelled drive, a shuffling and muttering and self-conscious whisperings, a momentary silence — and then the bursting forth on the sharp air of a score of voices, at first with doubtful unison but soon with growing confidence and discipline:

> Hark! the herald angels sing
> Glory to the new-born King,
> Peace on earth, and mercy mild,
> God and sinners reconciled . . .

It was the Youth Club, under the tutelage of Dan Figgins, making its annual carol-singing tour of the parish, this year in aid of a cancer fund, and every night for the next three weeks before Christmas they will do their rounds, in fine weather or foul. As with the work of Mr Slocum's helpers, their singing went with an even better swing after we had plied them gratefully with spiced-up scrumpy.

One of the chief contributors to village activities is the Women's Institute. It is, of course, active throughout the year and plays a considerable part in village affairs. In spite of all the repetitive music-hall jokes, it is a worthy body (its origins were in Canada sixty-odd years ago) and its monthly meetings do not just consist of idiocies such as competitions to see how many different items can be contained in a match-box — reminiscent of mediaeval speculation about how many angels could be accommodated on the head of a pin. They have speakers on a variety of subjects from the work of the police to Roman remains in the county, and from time to time some of our local luminaries (they don't expect a fee) are invited to give a talk — the ex-bank manager on his world cruise, complete with slides, or Miss Bundy on the fern-garden, or Captain RN with a stirringly blue-nosed but self-censored account of conditions in the region of Bear Island. They run courses on needlework, spinning and dyeing, and they hold coffee mornings and charity jumble sales (the Rector claims that he had to buy back a pair of his best trousers his wife had sacrificed). And possibly because the Squire's lady is president, all the other ladies of the village are members, not forgetting the wives of some of the farmers and various other villagers. But not all the younger women belong, with children coming home from school or husbands from work, and a debate is in progress as to whether the meetings should take place in the afternoon or evening, while for some of them, devotees of women's magazines, 'Institute' may have a dated ring.

By origin, the turkey, so familiar an item on our Christmas table, is an American bird. Apart from dogs, turkeys were the only domesticated animals kept by the Aztecs, and the sixteenth-century explorer Cortez described them as 'peacocks', saying that hundreds of them wandered about the royal palaces.

But it is for its Christmas party that the WI is best known in the village, for at this function every member has the right to bring a guest — mostly husbands. So, half the male population, willy-nilly, is expected to turn up. Actually, we do so gladly, for it is all a very uninhibited, jolly affair, which is helped to run smoothly because the WI starts off with supper and insists on the old-fashioned country practice of seating everyone on benches at a hugely long trestle table stretching almost the length of the village hall — instead of the more sophisticated separate tables favoured by the Amateur Dramatic Society, with candles in bottles modishly encrusted in wax.

It is as well that those trestles are solidly made, for the tables, covered with snow-white cloths, are spread with enough good victuals to satisfy a whole regiment of Parson Woodfordes and fat boys of Dingley Dell. The *pièce de résistance* is an enormous turkey, which might have been the cause of some slight acrimony, one member of the Christmas Party Committee having taken it upon herself to ask the ex-bank manager to carve, while someone else had complicated matters by asking the Fleckham accountant. However, the Rector, with his customary good-humoured diplomacy, suggested that the President's guest (laughter) should be invited to do the honours (hear, hear), whereupon the Squire, making the carving knife and fork glitter dramatically, proceeded to slice up the turkey under a battery of critical eyes, remarking that he had never expected to be given the bird by the Women's Institute (much more laughter).

And by the time the mince-pies and the jellies make their appearance, and the crackers have been pulled and everybody is happily wearing a comic hat or a false nose or blowing paper trumpets or reading out jokes and riddles, and some of the old people such as Sam Dredge and Mrs Slee are positively glowing with all the good food they have packed in, the hall is in a companionable uproar, despite the fact that the only stimulant has been mahogany coloured tea strong enough to trot a mouse on. Then, when everything has been cleared away and the benches put back around the walls and the trestle tables dismantled by Fred Marks and Jack Farley, we indulge in those games which are as homely as apple-crumble and which nowadays you find only at WI parties — and not always then.

Favourite among these games is undoubtedly passing-the-parcel, for with the forfeit entailed for being stuck with the parcel when Miss Bundy's strummings on the piano cease, there is always the chance of some village dignitary being the victim. A certain amount of sharp practice, or, shall we say, last-minute passing goes on in the hope that someone like the Rector or the Squire has the confounded parcel dumped in his lap when the music stops. Eagerly we watch to see how they will acquit themselves when called to perform some ludicrous act.

The Rector, made to talk for a minute, says they have picked the wrong person — it's a cinch for him, claiming that he is an ecclesiastical Clement Freud. The Squire fares worse, being made to peel an orange blindfold, and Mrs Endacott next to him tut-tuts as his flowered waistcoat suffers. As for Mr Maundy-Hansom, the shy young architect, when his forfeit ordained that he should kiss his favourite person in the room, he gallantly, if blushingly, delivered a chaste salute on the wrinkled cheek of the sexton's wife, which induced a warm cheer, and an 'Oh my!' from Mrs Endacott, who clearly would have relished being in Mrs Doe's place.

But the forfeit that brought instant response and success was when George Huggins, the AA scout, was required to sing a song. He needed no urging and, springing to his feet, with hands crossed in front of him, his eyes bulging, his neck swelling, delivered a stentorian rendering of 'The Cheerful Horn':

> The cheerful 'orn he blaws in the morn,
> And we'll a-'untin' goo;

'What passion cannot music raise and quell!', Dryden rightly said.
But the trumpet's loud clangour doesn't necessarily
excite us to arms!

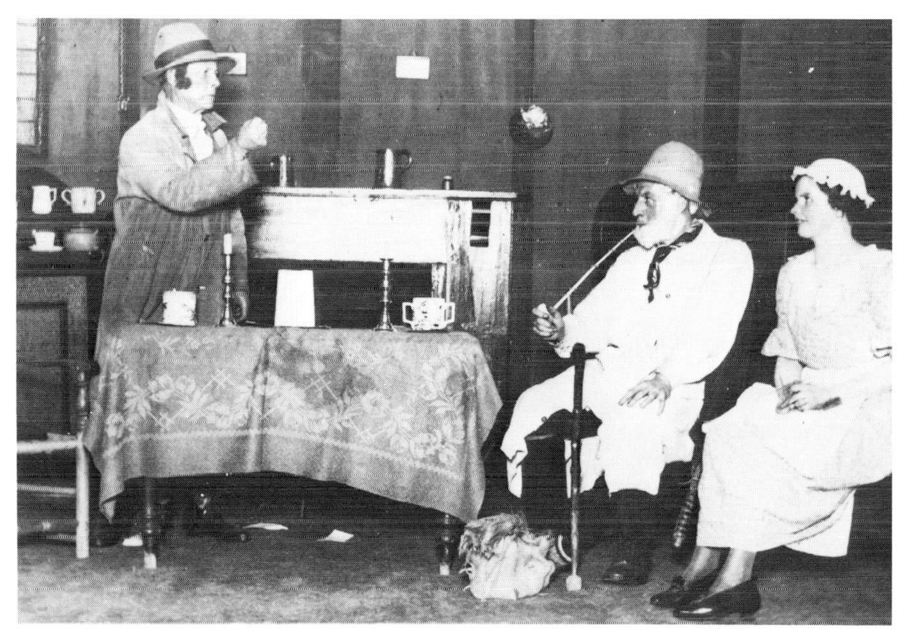

All the world's a stage,
And all the men and women merely players;
They have their exits and their entrances
And one man in his time plays many parts.

Do we love dressing up and creating another world, however
temporary, because real life is so fraught and humdrum?

Christmas is everywhere the most popular festival of the whole year, combining as it does the religious and social sides of life in a way none of the other ecclesiastical Holy-days do. The Church with its message of "Peace on earth, goodwill towards men", as it were, comes down and takes the hand of the people and says let us unite together to celebrate the mystery of family life at the altar of the home. Hence it appeals more forcibly than any other festival to young and old, rich and poor, town-dweller and country rustic, without distinction of creed or class.

ELIZABETH MARY WRIGHT, *Rustic Speech and Folk-lore* (1913)

The cheerful 'orn 'er blaws in the morn,
  And we'll a-'untin' goo,
    And we'll a-'untin' goo . . .
Vor all my fancy dwells upon Nancy,
  And I'll zing Tally-ho!
Vor all my vancy dwells upon Nancy,
  And I'll zing Tally-ho!

— and Miss Bundy, galloping in two bars behind, overtook him and struck up a spirited accompaniment. George would cheerfully have gone on 'ornin' through the remaining six verses had his jacket not been unceremoniously yanked by his wife.

After a stirring if somewhat overwhelming performance on the handbells by a team from Fleckham, the party ended with a sketch performed by members of the WI and written by Mrs Wise, the honorary secretary. Slyly remembering the recent performance of *Blithe Spirit* by the Amateur Dramatic Society, when a fearful bout of drying-up had occurred, she had made her heroine the prompter who eventually was obliged to jump up on the stage to take control of the proceedings. 'As good as any Whitehall farce,' the local paper subsequently reported.

And the Squire proposed a vote of thanks, remarking what a marvellous social cement a good WI provided.

Some village entertainments of course are private, but nonetheless typical for that. Now, before the advent of myxomatosis there were some fields in the parish where the rabbits were so numerous they seemed to move like a tawny shadow across the grass. The villagers reckoned the rabbits had to sleep in shifts, there were so many of them. Some farmers made considerable sums out of trapping, and when Fleckham station was still in use you could see scores of rabbit carcasses being dispatched to London every week.

It was generally agreed that there were far too many rabbits in the country altogether — partly because so many of their natural predators had been killed, partly because the people with trapping interests did not want the rabbit population reduced. Indeed, when 'myxie' did drastically bring this about, there was an hysterical search for a scapegoat. Absurd stories were printed in local newspapers about the vicious attacks by buzzards after they had been deprived of their favourite prey, young rabbits. There were even tarrydiddles about babies being attacked in their prams and of lorry-drivers afraid to collect the milk-churns because of the threatening behaviour of buzzards.

But the 'real' farmers rejoiced at the thinning-out of the rabbits, which had always done immense damage to banks, fouled grassland and consumed huge amounts of grass — ten rabbits ate as much as one sheep. After the first devastating outbreak of the disease, some farmers were able to pasture cattle in certain fields for the first time in years. There could be no two opinions about the disease itself, however. When, about a quarter of a century ago, myxomatosis first arrived in the parish, it was a ghastly affair. Everywhere you went, through meadow or copse, along the Drover's Way and even occasionally along the village 'back lanes', you came across the wretched animals, head and hind-quarters swollen grotesquely, humpling along blindly, actually bumping against your feet before you could put them out of their misery.

For a time the disease put an end to what for generations had been a Boxing

Pliny the Elder called the ferret *viverra*. Isidore of Seville named it *furo*, from the Latin for thief. What these Boxing Day sportsmen are calling it is probably unprintable.

Day tradition in the countryside — ferreting; centuries, possibly, rather than generations, for ferreting was a sport before the invention of the gun and there are references in documents of Richard II's reign to licences for ferreting. Then, after the first grisly wave, the disease came and went in periodical bouts, coupled with the fact that some rabbits developed an immunity to it. So this year, that staunch traditionalist, Mr Slocum, announced with satisfaction that 'I be going to du some ferretin' Boxing Morn, midear!'

That, we knew, meant a beery little picnic for half a dozen of Farmer Slocum's cronies, simply, it will be appreciated, as a pick-me-up after the intake of Christmas Day itself. It was a gathering of the select, for you had to be a first-class shot at ferreting. You couldn't just blaze away as they did in the syndicate's shoot when the cocks came high over. At ferreting you never had a chance of more than a reflex snap-shot, as an emerging rabbit bolted from one burrow to another.

'And you got tu hit 'un in the vore-parts,' warns Mr Slocum, earnestly. 'Hit a rabbit in the backside and 'er'll just crawl away to die in misery, poor creature, and you'll have the ferret lying up with 'un all day till she's dug out!'

And anybody who has ever been ferreting knows there is nothing worse for the temper than having to dig out a ferret, quite apart from the back-breaking labour entailed.

'But they'll bolt sure enough this morning,' Mr Slocum declares, as we assemble near the Plague Ground. 'Did 'ee zee the weather-vane on the church debating the matter? 'Tis going to turn cold, I rackon, and that always makes the rabbits more frisky, zno?'

With familiar confidence he puts a hand in the bag and brings out a musky-smelling, pale yellow, pink-eyed ferret, so docile you wonder that it is one of the most blood-thirsty animals in existence, its small, impeccably white teeth lethal weapons, especially once they have drawn blood. Scarcely has it gone snaking into the burrow and Mr Slocum hurried out into the field than the first rabbit bolts.

And scarcely has it done so when the first shot rings out, shattering the biting air. Head over heels goes the rabbit, a clean kill, and at the bolt hole the ferret appears briefly, small head wavering delicately, as if to ask whether it was doing its job all right, before vanishing again into the earthy darkness to spread its message of death among the long-eared colony.

So it goes on all morning, through the broad acres of Town Farm, and the farmers and their sons did not let the ferret down. With the best of them, their guns seemed to be part of themselves. No time to voice the equivalent of 'My bird, I think!' They shot instinctively and, as if well aware of the fact that there still aren't all that many rabbits, few chances are missed. Besides, with cartridges the price they are, you can't afford to miss. And anyway, they are constantly keeping their hand in at the wood-pigeon or even clay-pigeon shooting.

By the time Gertie Slocum drove up in the Land-Rover with the beer and sandwiches to the appointed *rendezvous*, ten rabbits had been knocked over.

''Tis quite like old times, midear,' Mr Slocum beams, sitting on a fallen log and sinking his teeth into an enormous beef sandwich, with a mug of beer in the other hand. 'But, my dear soul, Gertie! Drat the maid, I du believe she has gone and forgot the mustard!'

Some village entertainments are quite fortuitous and only rarely occur. Abruptly, in the dramatic way we are acquainted with in this country, the weather does a complete turnabout exactly as Mr Slocum had forecast. One day the golden cockerel on the church tower is blankly surveying the douce south-west which had allowed us to leave off our overcoats; next, he is shimmering in the gem-hard light that comes with the east wind.

Newspapers are draped over geraniums in many a glass porch. From a distance half a hundred chimneys make the centre of the village resemble in miniature the dark satanic mills of yesteryear. In Slocum's bullock-yard the animals are almost invisible in their own steam. Hussey's sheep tittup along his iron-hard lane with a delicate rattling of feet. The agonized squealing of hungry pigs increases in direct proportion with the cold. Disconsolate feathered supplicants crowd the bird-tables. Redwings and fieldfares take off farther west. Somebody claims to have seen a brambling. Woodcock have been reported in Frog's Bottom. Miss Bundy counted eighteen wrens roosting in a nesting-box. At night the cries of mating foxes add to the atmosphere of frosty desolation.

And the Drover's Pond freezes over.

The first intimation of that is the triumphant whoops of village children, whose iconoclastic spirit responds instantly. 'Smash the enemy!' they seem to be saying. 'Stone him dead!' The occasional wettings before the ice freezes over right to the edge discourages some of them, but, in addition, the Brigadier's soldier-son, on leave from Germany, has been alerted.

Somewhat like Mr Wardle with Mr Pickwick, he persuades the iconoclasts that sliding (none possesses skates) can be infinitely more fun than playing ducks and drakes with stones that stick to the ice and spoil it for real skating. (Mr Pickwick 'took two or three short runs, baulked himself as often, and at last took another run, and went slowly and gravely down the slide, with his feet about a yard and a quarter apart, amidst the gratified shouts of all the spectators'.) The young Captain then proceeds to evoke their admiration with some real Robin Cousins stuff, and, when the Squire's niece arrives on the scene, he and she put on a joint turn which Mr Maundy-Hansom, ever romantic, says looks exactly like Levin and Kitty skating together in *Anna Karenina*.

Others have discovered cumbersome old skates in forgotten cupboards or lofts. Miss Rix, ever game, brings a kitchen chair to push in front of her as a support. Captain RN does a jaunty turn or two, hands behind back, before his steering gear develops a fault and he founders spectacularly on to the creaking ice. Cheerfully he accepts a brawny helping hand from Alf Whittle, with whom he hasn't been on speaking terms since that business of the pump and the village green.

Some of the older boys have rapidly learned the joys of sliding and in imitation of the Captain (soldier, not RN), one of them indulges in some ambitious work Sam Weller would have approved — he called it knocking at the cobbler's shop, and it consisted of skimming over the ice on one foot, while every now and then giving a postman's knock on it with the other.

By Saturday afternoon half the village comes to join in the fun, either actively or passively. Alf Whittle has gone in especially to the big town to buy a pair of skates, and by sheer doggedness and strength teaches himself to skate, unmindful of all the falls and bruisings he endures, for he is built like a Rugby League forward and has a great tyre of fleshy padding all over before you get to the bones.

And Mr Bragham simply cannot resist such an occasion! Not to skate — he knows his limitations — but with that self-same brazier that did duty at the wassailing party almost a year ago. With the help of Jeremy Dredge and Fred Marks, he gets it going, so that its cheerful light flickers over the ice, while Mrs Bragham and her helpers are not far behind with supplies of mince-pies.

Long after the molten sun, fiercely blazing its indignation at the affronting cold, has sunk behind Starvation Hill, the strident fun continues:

> So through the darkness and the cold we flew.
> And not a voice was idle.
> It was a time of rapture! Clear and loud
> The village clock tolled six, — I wheeled about,
> Proud and exulting like an untired horse
> That cares not for his home. All shod with steel,
> We hissed along the polished ice in games
> Confederate, imitative of the chase . . .

The village was joyfully taking advantage of this God-given opportunity, and, though we don't lack our squabbles and pettinesses and idiocies and prejudices and all those other faults catalogued by William Hazlitt, this was one of the occasions on which that special matiness of a village community comes through. No longer is the village the self-contained entity of old, but there is still, at times, a feeling of community, a certain identity, that has not been completely stifled by the drear anonymity and indifference of modern life. The ice on the Drover's Pond that weekend was thick enough to support all our harmless caperings and antics and allow us for a moment to forget that much thinner ice the world is constantly skating on.

BIBLIOGRAPHY

Bonham-Carter, V., *The English Village* (London 1952)
Bourne, G., *Change in the Village* (London 1912); *A Farmer's Life* (London 1922)
Bovill, E.W., *English Country Life* 1780–1830 (London 1962)
Byng, Hon. J., *The Torrington Diaries* (London 1934)
Cobbett, W., *Cottage Economy* (London 1828); *Rural Rides* (London 1830)
de la Mare, W., *Come Hither* (London 1923)
Grigson, G., *An English Farmhouse* (London 1948)
Hardy, T., *The Return of the Native* (London 1878); *The Woodlanders* (London 1887)
Hazlitt, W., *Essay on Wordsworth's "The Excursion"* (London 1820)
Hudson, W.H., *A Shepherd's Life* (London 1910)
Martin, E.W., *The Secret People* (London 1952)
Massingham, H.J., *Country Relics* (Cambridge 1939)
Mitford, M., *Our Village* (London 1824–32)
Raymond, W., *English Country Life* (Edinburgh 1910)
Sassoon, S., *Memoirs of a Fox-hunting Man* (London 1928)
Surtees, R.S., *Mr Sponge's Sporting-tour* (London 1854)
Thompson, F., *Lark Rise to Candleford* (Oxford 1945)
Trevelyan, G.M., *English Social History* (London 1942)
Tusser, T., *500 Pointes of Good Husbandrie* (1573)
Young, A., *A Tour through the Southern Counties of England* (1769)

ACKNOWLEDGEMENTS

The author and publishers would like to thank the following for supplying illustrations:

Colour

Aquila Photographics 33, 105; Eric Bawden 34(above), 40(above), 106(above), 110; Janet and Colin Bord 36, 111; Chris Chapman 109; Richard and Sally Greenhill 112(below); Archie Miles 35; James Ravilious 34(below), 38/9, 40(below), 106(below), 107, 112 (above); John Topham Picture Library 37, 108.

Black and white

Aquila Photographics 66; Chris Chapman 61; Richard and Sally Greenhill 46/7, 58(above), 87, 133(above), 143, 154(below); Hereford City Library 78; Institute of Agricultural History and Museum of English Rural Life, University of Reading 58(below), 100, 122, 153(below); James Ravilious 2/3, 11, 12, 15, 18/19, 25, 26, 28/9, 45, 48(below), 57, 69(above), 70, 75, 79, 88/9, 93, 94, 113, 114(below), 121, 123, 125, 129, 130, 133(below), 139, 140, 141, 144, 150/51, 153(above), 154(above); John Topham Picture Library 48(above), 69(below), 102/3, 114(above); George Tucker 82/3, 156; R. Willbie 55.

Thanks are due to Nigel Nicolson Esq. for permission to quote lines from *The Land* by Victoria Sackville-West and to the Oxford University Press for permission to quote from *English Country Life, 1780–1830* by the late E.W. Bovill.

INDEX

Page numbers in *italic* type indicate illustrations

amateur Dramatics 135, 152, *153*, 155

beekeeping *78–9*, 132
Belloc, Hilaire 146
bell-ringers 8–10, *11*
blacksmith *37*, 42, 67
Bourne, George 61, 62, 78, 80
Bovill, E.W. 24, 27, 142
Bow Street Runners 27
Bragham, Mr 10, 13, 14, 49, 71, 131, 158
brewing, 134
Bridges, Robert 10
Brigadier, the 8, 13–16, 24, 42, 49, 71, 72
Broad Halfpenny Down 98
Broomball cutting 59–60

Captain RN 9, 14, 49, 51, 71, 118
Carew, William 144
carnival 134–6
carol singing 149, *154*
Chesterton, G.K. 145
church, churchyard 8, 9, 16, *18–19*, 42–9, *45*, *46–7*, 48, 124
cider, cider-making 13, 14, 128–32, *129*
Civil War 142
Clare, John 16, 49, 126
Cobbett, William, 22, 27, 62, 84, 95, 96, 134, 142
Coke of Norfolk 50
Comstock, Albert, gamekeeper 23–4, 32, 74, 84
Corn Laws 24
Counter, Mr, ex-bank manager 9, 51–2, 71, 98, 101
County Council 52, 91
Coverley, Sir Roger de 50
cricket 98–101, *102*, 104, 115–16
Cupani, Brother 81

Darnley Copse 24
Darwin, Charles 44
Deedes, Mr, Parish Council chairman 8, 51–2, 71
De la Mare, Walter 92, 128
Dickens, Charles 50, 61, 115
District Council 20, 42, 52, 91
Doe, Cushy, sexton 16, 23, 42, 90, 104
dominoes 23
dowsing *see* water-divining
Dredge, Jeremy 8, 20, 119, 138
Dredge, Reg 9, 44, 67, 73, 98, 99
Dredge, Sam 8–10, 14, 22–4, 30–32, 51 60–62, 120
Drovers' Lea 62, 76, 77
Drovers' Pond 118, 157, 158
Drovers' Road 20, 42, 49, 54, 59–62, 74, 155
Dunch, Mrs 16, 20, 42

Education Act 96
enclosures 76–80
Endacott, Mrs 90, 98, 120
entertainments, village 118–20, 148–58

farm animals 17, *36*, 64–5, 86, *87*, *88–9*, 90–91, *114*
farming (various) *12*, *25*, *57*, 64–5, *66*, *69*, *109*
ferreting 155–7, *156*
field names 74, 76
Figgins, Dan 8, 13–14
flail 95, 96
Fleckham 64, 71, 95, 115, 134, 135, 136
Flower Show 90, 118–20, *121*
'Fly-blow' 86, 90
Fishing *61*, 71, 72
football *34*, 142–5
footpaths 74–7
Forster, W.E., Education Minister 96

fox-hunting, *38–9*, 138 *et seq.*, *140–41*, 142
Fuller, Thomas 9
funeral 42, 43

gamekeeper *see* Comstock
Garden Club 118
garden pests 84
Gaskell, Mrs 119
Gimblett, Harold 116
goose plucking 149
gypsies 126, *143*

Hardy, Thomas 44, 65–7, 131
harriers 142
Harvest Festival *45*, *112*, 123–4, *133*
harvest home 120–23
Hawker, Col Peter 27, 30
Hazlitt, William 118, 120, 148, 158
Herrick, Robert 16
highwaymen 62
Hoggett, Jack, farmer 86, 90
Home Farm 128
Hopkins, Gerard Manley 91
'howlers' 13–14
Hudson, W.H., 27, 50
Hussey, George, farmer 86, 126

Johnson, Dr Samuel 145

Kalevala, the 68
Keane, PC 8, 86, 90, 101

Lamb, The (village inn) 8, 9, 20, 22, 23, 32, 44, 64, 71, 86, 101, 138
lambing 10, 17, 18

Macdonnell, A.G. 115
Maiden Castle 120
market-stall *28–9*
Masefield, John 43
Maundy-Hansom, Mr, architect 71, 119, 135, 136
maximus 9
mead 132, 134
Methodist minister 145
Meynell, Hugo 142
Mitford, Mary 17, 30, 60, 115–16
myxomatosis 155, 156

newcomers 22
nutting 126
Nut-tree Corner, cottage 22, 132

Parish Council 8, 42, 50–52, 71, 74, 76, 77, 91, 98, 101, 128, 144
Plague Ground 76, 92, 156
Playing Fields Association 144
poaching 23 *et seq.*
point-to-point 54–8
Portsmouth, Lord 30
Post Office, village 128
pump, village 50–52

railway 59, 60
Ray, John 84
Rector 10, 13,14, 42, 44, 101, 104, 118
Richard II 156
river-bailiff 31
Rix, Miss *see* village school
Rural Rides 27

Sackville, Lord John 115
Sackville-West, Victoria 128
saddler 68
St John, Charles 30
salmon 30, 31, 69, 71

Sassoon, Siegfried 115, 119
Saxons 132
Scrope, William 72
seine-netting 68, 71, 72
sexton, *see* Doe, Cushy
Shaddock, Percy 54, 138
shepherd *12*, *66*, *69*, *109*
shop, village 17, 124
silver band 119, 135, 136
skating *154*, 157, 158
Slocum, farmer & family 13–17, 51, 64, 72, 74, 86, 90, 119, 126–8, 131, 148, 155–7
Smith, Sydney 27
'snow-bones' 16
Sportsman's Directory, The 142
Squire 22, 49, 50, 84, 98, *100*, 104, 126, 128, 155
Starvation Hill 10, 17, 54, 55, 92, 158
Surtees, R.S., quoted 54–5, 59, 61, 139
'Swing, Captain' 24

thatcher, thatching 22, 65–7, *122–3*
Thompson, Flora 44
Thompson, James quoted 59
Thornback, George, farmer 64–5, 128
tithes 44, 49
Tolstoi, Leo 50, 158
Town Farm *see* Slocum
Townsend, Turnip 50
Trevelyan, G.M. 64, 115
Trollope, Anthony, quoted 86, 142
Tull, Jethro 50
Tusser, Thomas 77, 120

UDS (salmon disease) 71

village fields 74, 76
village gardens 80 *et seq.*, *82–3*, *106*, 118, 119, *130*
village fields 74, 76
Village Hall 118–20, 152
village lanes 90–95
village pound 91
village scenes *12*, *15*, *35*, 69, *75*, *94*, *121*, *125*, *144*, *154*
village school & children *40*, *48*, *58*, *61*, 92–6, *93*
village shop 17, 124, 148
village sports 119,120

Wagner, Richard 68
Walton, Izaak 72
wassailing 13–16
Watchet, Mr, Parish Council clerk 13, 23, 98
water-divining 95
White, 'Farmer' 116
Whittle, Alf, lorry-driver 44, 51, 157
wild animals *33*, *105*
wild flowers, fruits 90, 92, 94, 124, 126
Women's Institute 13, *28*, *29*, 49, 92, 118, 148, 149, 152
Woodforde, Parson 152
Wordsworth, William 43, 148, 158

Young, Arthur 77
Young Farmers' Club 128
Youth Club 149